The Way to FREEDOM

Breaking Through Inner Fears and
Unfolding the Strength of Vulnerability

BETHSAIDA HINGSTON

First published by Ultimate World Publishing 2025
Copyright © 2025 Bethsaida Hingston

ISBN

Paperback: 978-1-923425-15-6
Ebook: 978-1-923425-16-3

Bethsaida Hingston has asserted her rights under the Copyright, Designs and Patents Act 1988 to be identified as the author of this work. The information in this book is based on the author's experiences and opinions. The publisher specifically disclaims responsibility for any adverse consequences which may result from use of the information contained herein. Permission to use information has been sought by the author. Any breaches will be rectified in further editions of the book.

All rights reserved. No part of this publication may be reproduced, stored in or introduced into a retrieval system, or transmitted in any form, or by any means (electronic, mechanical, photocopying, recording or otherwise) without the prior written permission of the author. Any person who does any unauthorised act in relation to this publication may be liable to criminal prosecution and civil claims for damages. Enquiries should be made through the publisher.

Cover design: Ultimate World Publishing
Layout and typesetting: Ultimate World Publishing
Editor: Maddie Johnson

Ultimate World Publishing
Diamond Creek,
Victoria Australia 3089
www.writeabook.com.au

Testimonials

I am honoured that (Betsy) Bethsaida has asked me to share a few words as she celebrates the completion of her book.

Our friendship began about 26 years ago when she arrived in Darwin, NT, Australia—newly married, pregnant with her first child, and beginning life in a new country. Her zest for life, natural warmth, and unwavering cheerfulness shone through, and we quickly became close friends, bonded by our faith and love of family.

Not long after, Betsy launched her Mexican food truck at the Mindil Beach Sunset Markets, and on those evenings, we would care for baby Deborah at our home. It was evident from the start that Betsy had an entrepreneurial spirit and wasn't afraid to take on new challenges.

As her family grew to four children, we shared in the joy of each birth, waiting at home with the older siblings, eagerly anticipating each new arrival. Family has always been at the heart of Betsy's life. We loved visiting her Humpty Doo property, where she raised farm animals, experimented with gardening, and worked on various house projects. We'd help where we could, enjoying homemade Mexican meals and learning cooking tips along the way.

Through the years, we also shared bittersweet farewells as Betsy and her family moved interstate for work and later returned to her beloved Mexico before ultimately deciding to settle once again in the Top End. Throughout these transitions—and even through the pain of a difficult marriage breakup—Betsy remained determined. She mastered English, pursued continuous learning to expand her skills, and worked tirelessly to support her family and serve her community. Her personal and family experiences have deeply influenced her studies and career path.

One memory that stands out is during one of Betsy's house moves, when we all sat in a circle on the bare living room floor, eating pizza because there was no furniture yet. The space was filled with laughter, and Betsy's infectious optimism and enthusiasm for a fresh start set the tone for the journey ahead.

Years have passed, and we have both grown older—hopefully wiser. Now grandmothers, we continue to marvel at Betsy's incredible work ethic, ambition, and relentless drive to make the most of her time on this earth.

We eagerly look forward to reading her book and wish her every success and happiness in her business ventures and life's adventures. Betsy will always be a treasured friend and an inspiration.

- Robyn Kuhn
(Retired Primary School Teacher, Dip. B Ed.)
& Michael Kuhn (Retired Managing Director,
Building Company)

I can recall memories from as far back as when I was just three or four years old. Over the years, I have witnessed my mother's journey—the highs of her successes and the depths of her struggles, including the darkest moments that, in hindsight, served as powerful life lessons. These experiences have contributed not only to my mother's personal and spiritual growth but also to my own.

Before I continue, I want to share something important with those reading this. I have always reminded my mum— never give up! I cannot stress this enough.

"Keep your circle of friends small and tight. Never ignore your intuition, because there are always lessons to be learned. If something feels off from the start, trust that feeling. Unfortunately, not everyone has good intentions— sometimes, those we trust most, whether a partner or a best friend, may not have our best interests at heart. There will always be snakes in the grass, but there is also always room for us to grow and improve."

For the past 26 years, I have not only been a witness but also a participant in these life-changing experiences alongside my mother. Through her, and through my own journey, I have learned that sometimes we must endure heartbreak, financial struggles, emotional turmoil, and even mental battles that push us to our limits.

But what I have also learned—through experience and faith—is that with the right mindset, doors will always open. And if a door doesn't open, then a window will crack just enough for us to find our way through. The right opportunities are always within reach when we commit to working hard, stay resilient, and push ourselves beyond our limits.

I call this realization my "third eye awakening." My mother played a significant role in triggering this for me, but I wouldn't have found my true path without the guidance of two remarkable women: the incredible Cassandra Hurley and my own mother, Bethsaida Hingston—also known as Betsy, Bettyz. These two strong and inspiring women have helped me find my direction and navigate life's challenges with wisdom and courage.

I have loved watching my mother's growth, and I aspire to make a name for myself just as she has.

Thank you, Mum.

- **Deborah Hingston**
A proud mother of four exceptional children and a mother who never gives up

I, Asenat Flores Cabrera, am grateful to have witnessed my sister Bethsaida's journey from childhood to the remarkable woman she is today. Her unwavering dedication and determination to achieve her goals have always impressed me.

I remember her younger years vividly—always optimistic, always striving to change the world around her. Her educational achievements played a significant role in shaping her path, and from an early age, she aspired to become someone who would inspire others.

Bethsaida has always possessed a strong, determined spirit, insisting on doing things her way. Her choices, though sometimes challenging, have ultimately shaped her into the person she is today—someone of great significance to those around her. One of the most profound influences in her life was her relationship with our father, Filemon Flores Velasco. Though she may not have openly expressed it at the time, it was a source of strength that helped her develop the courage to stand by her beliefs and question the things that didn't align with them.

Today, I couldn't be prouder of Bethsaida as she takes a bold step toward sharing her lifelong dreams with the world through her book.

- Asenat Flores Cabrera
Systems Engineer | Founder & Business Owner,
Flores y Detalles, Mexico

I have worked with Bethsaida Hingston since 2021, when I first launched my business. Over the years, I have stood by her side, watching her grow, expand, and become more self-aware. She has put in the hard work to better herself and has even begun her own life coaching journey.

Bethsaida didn't just learn—she embraced transformation, evolving into an inspiration for so many others. Her journey hasn't been easy, but we've worked through past traumas together, and she has emerged stronger than ever.

She never let anything stand in the way of her dreams. No matter the obstacles, she remained determined to pursue her path. Bethsaida is one of the sweetest, kindest souls I know, and I am beyond proud to call her my client.

I am incredibly excited for her future because I know that this book is just the beginning.

I LOVE YOU, QUEEN! I have no doubt that you will continue to change lives—for the better!

- XO-Cass LLC
Cassandra Hurley, CEO
Psychic Medium & Worldwide Life Coach

Dedication

To my family and friends, and to <u>any of</u> those who have felt lost, burdened, or trapped in the shadows of their own emotions.

I dedicate these words to the seekers—those who, despite their pain, continue to search for light. In moments of doubt, may you find hope within these pages. Know that emotional freedom is not a distant dream but a path you can walk, step by step, even in the hardest of times.

I also write these words to those who struggle in silence, hoping they serve as a guide toward finding light, even in the darkest places. May you discover the courage to reclaim your story, walk the path of emotional freedom, and know that you are never alone.

Contents

Testimonials	iii
Dedication	xi
Preface	1
Introduction	3
CHAPTER I: My self-abandonment	7
CHAPTER II: Emotional transformation against my unknown	19
CHAPTER III: The power against enmeshment	25
CHAPTER IV: The silent war: Heart vs mind	31
CHAPTER V: Causality or Reality	43
CHAPTER VI: Fear of self-reclamation?	47
CHAPTER VII: Echoes of the frozen summit	61
CHAPTER VIII: My consciousness after a journey of healing	73
CHAPTER IX: Uncertainty as a mask	85
CHAPTER X: I Trusted You!	99
CHAPER XI: Practical Tools for Self-Connection After Consequential Self-Dishonour	113
CHAPTER XII: Time and potential—vital life forces wanting to break free	121

CHAPTER XIII: My Terms, My Conditions, My Loss	137
Conclusion	149
About The Author	153
Acknowledgements	155
References	157
Speaker Bio	161

Preface

Freedom. It is a word we all long for, yet often struggle to fully grasp. We seek it in our external lives—through career changes, relationships, or physical escapes.

But what if true freedom isn't something we can find "out there"? What if it is something we must first discover within ourselves?

In writing *The Way to Freedom*, I wanted to share the journey that led me to understand that freedom is not the absence of obstacles, but the liberation from the internal forces that hold us back. Throughout my life, I found myself caught in cycles of fear, doubt, and confusion—feeling trapped by expectations, both external and internal. It wasn't until I began to explore the inner landscapes of my mind and spirit that I realised the key to real freedom lies in shedding these limiting beliefs and returning to my true, unshackled self.

This book is the culmination of that exploration. It is a guide to help you step beyond the confines of your conditioned mind and embrace a life where you are no longer a prisoner to fear, insecurity, or the past. It's not just a collection of ideas—it's a call to action. Within these pages, you will find tools, practices, and reflections that can help you break free from whatever holds you back, whether that be self-doubt, negative thought patterns, or societal pressures.

Each chapter is meant to take you on a journey—not just of discovery, but of transformation. The principles I share here have helped me shift my perspective and experience life in a way that feels lighter, more aligned, and deeply meaningful. It is my hope that by reading this book, you too will come to see that freedom is not a distant goal, but a reality that you can begin to embrace right now.

As you read, I encourage you to reflect, to question, and most importantly, to practice. Freedom is a process, not a one-time event. It is something we must actively choose every day, every moment. This book is not meant to be a destination, but a stepping stones on your own path to greater peace, joy, and authentic living.

Thank you for allowing me to be part of your journey. I hope *The Way to Freedom* serves as a guide, a companion, and a reminder that true liberation is already within your reach.

With gratitude,
Bethsaida Hingston

Introduction

My dear reader,

This book is more than words on a page; it is a reflection of my journey through life's most challenging and transformative moments. I have walked paths of joy, love, loss, and rediscovery, and through it all, I have learned that the road to healing and growth is never linear.

As I share my journey with you, it is my hope that you find pieces of your own experiences woven between the lines. Life has a way of teaching lessons in unexpected ways. By opening my heart, I hope to inspire, comfort, and remind you that no matter where you are on your journey, there is always hope and a path forward. I invite you to walk with me through the highs and lows. Perhaps, through my story, you'll find the opportunity to reflect on your own strengths and discover the hope that lies beyond every challenge.

Life has a way of leading us down paths we never expected to walk. For years, I journeyed through the highs and lows of a marriage that shaped much of who I believed I was as a spouse, partner, and companion. When that chapter came to an end, it felt like the ground had fallen away beneath my feet. Divorce can feel like a loss of identity, dreams, and the life you once imagined. When my marriage ended, I was confronted with a daunting question: Who am I now? But as I began to rebuild my life, I discovered something extraordinary—hope.

This book is not about the pain of separation but the transformation that can follow. It's a testament to our resilience, even when it feels buried beneath the weight of sorrow. I've learned that hope doesn't always appear as a bright light in the distance; sometimes, it's a flicker, a quiet whisper urging us to keep going.

And that's enough.

As I found my way to freedom and healing, I realised that the end of one chapter can be the beginning of a beautiful new story.

It's never easy to say goodbye to a life you've built. The focus is on resilience and the idea that divorce, rather than breaking you, can become a source of strength and new beginnings.

Introduction

Divorce is often seen as the breaking point, the moment when life as you know it comes undone. But what if I told you that it is where true strength is born? What if this painful ending could become the starting point of a new and powerful chapter?

When I found myself at that crossroads, I didn't know what the future held. I was afraid. But through the pain and fear, I learned the most important lesson of all: I could rebuild, and there is always hope, even when the future feels uncertain.

Divorce brings with it a storm of emotions—grief, anger, confusion, and even relief. It can feel like the end of everything familiar. I know this because I've walked through that storm, unsure if I would ever find peace again. But through that journey, I discovered that even in heartbreak, hope exists. It might not appear in the way we expect, but it is there, quietly waiting to be found.

As you read these pages, I want you to know that you are not alone in your pain, and your feelings—no matter how complex—are valid. But more importantly, I hope these words bring you a sense of hope. Divorce was not the end of my story, and it doesn't have to be the end of yours. This journey is an opportunity to heal, grow, and step into a new chapter filled with possibilities. Your most extraordinary chapter may still be waiting to unfold. Hold on to hope, even in your darkest moments, because a brighter future lies ahead.

CHAPTER I

My self-abandonment

"We must accept finite disappointment but never lose infinite hope."
- Martin Luther King, Jr

"A whole stack of memories never equals one little hope."
- Charles M. Schulz

It was December 25, 2015, and I had yet to fully grasp the reality I was facing. When I walked into the living room, books were flying everywhere, and both familiar and unfamiliar faces filled the space. I had woken up after taking sleeping pills, hoping to escape the pain of my already broken and unlucky marriage.

For seventeen years, my inner world was a storm of unhappiness, a volatile environment created by a difficult marriage. My journey to emotional freedom, from those years and through divorce, was the most challenging and transformative experience of my life.

The abandonment I felt during my marriage slowly broke the connection I had with myself. As I dealt with emotional loneliness, I drifted further from who I used to be, losing my sense of self and confidence. The pain of feeling invisible and unheard created a gap within me that was even harder to close than the distance between us.

I was frozen by the fear of my marriage ending, knowing that criticism and judgment from religious circles would come quickly and harshly. Their traditional beliefs would place blame without understanding the silent struggles I was facing. It felt like their expectations mattered more than the pain I was enduring, or the emotional isolation and abandonment I was living through.

My self-abandonment

In religious and cultural settings, the fear of a marriage ending often stems from values instilled in us from a young age. Faith and tradition emphasise the sanctity and permanence of marriage, promoting the idea of a lifelong, strong, and harmonious bond. However, when a marriage begins to fall apart, it can bring overwhelming feelings of shame, guilt, and failure.

It was at this point that I started questioning myself.

i. *Have I noticed any signs of an emotionally unhealthy marriage or felt unnoticed for extended periods?*
The emotional distance was barely noticeable in the beginning—a missed conversation here, a postponed date there. Over the years, these small gaps widened, not through dramatic arguments but through a growing silence that filled our home. I remember evenings when we sat side by side, yet our minds were miles apart, each lost in our own separate worlds.

ii. *How does staying in an unhappy marriage impact self-worth and identity over time?*
Each day spent in that unhappy marriage chipped away at my confidence. I began questioning my worth, attributing every failure and frustration to my perceived shortcomings. The person I once was, the vibrant, hopeful individual, faded into the background, overshadowed by doubts.

iii. How do societal or religious expectations create additional pressure to stay in an unhappy marriage?
The conflict between personal happiness and external expectations highlighted the struggle between following my heart and adhering to external pressure. In my faith, marriage is a union between two people and a sacred covenant in God's eyes. Regardless of personal unhappiness, the expectation to remain steadfast weighed heavenly on me. Every contemplation of separation was met with silent disapproval, making the path to leaving feel not only personal, but spiritually fraught.

iv. What emotional and psychological impacts does abandonment within a marriage have on both partners?
The abandonment of the marital relationship impacted both of us emotionally, physically, and financially. Loneliness, rejection, and loss of connection were emotional withdrawals that left us invisible, as if our presence no longer mattered. The constant absence created a void that echoed with unanswered questions and unspoken pain. This abandonment wasn't just a gap in our relationship; it was a chasm that eroded the foundation of trust and love once built.

v. Why is it so difficult for individuals in unhealthy marriages to recognise their situation as toxic, and what helps break through that denial?

My self-abandonment

For years, I convinced myself that our struggles were temporary hurdles we could overcome. The hope that things would get better blinded me to the persistent patterns of disrespect and neglect. It wasn't until a particularly harsh argument that left me questioning my self-worth that I finally acknowledged the toxicity of our relationship.

vi. *How does living in an emotionally disconnected relationship impact the ability to connect with others outside the marriage?*

Isolation and emotional disconnection caused me to withdraw socially and develop trust issues rooted in past experiences. The emotional void at home made it even harder to reach out to friends and family. I felt too drained to socialise, and the fear of being vulnerable again kept me isolated. This disconnection spilled over into my interactions outside the marriage, making genuine connections feel both essential and frightening.

vii. *What are the long-term effects of staying in an unhealthy marriage on mental, emotional, and physical well-being?*

The prolonged stress of an unhealthy marriage took a toll on my mental and physical health. Sleepless nights were common, plagued by anxiety and relentless worry. Emotionally, I felt drained, unable to muster joy or enthusiasm for life. Physically, I noticed a decline in my health, with persistent headaches, fatigue, and a general sense of weariness that no amount of rest could alleviate.

viii. What roles do external judgments, such as those from religious or community groups, play in prolonging an unhealthy marriage?

The constant reminder from religious leaders that marriage was a lifelong commitment made me second-guess my desire to leave. The thought of being ostracised from my community from seeking a divorce was unbearable, pushing me to stay in a marriage that was slowly destroying me.

xix. How can someone start rebuilding their sense of self after experiencing emotional isolation or neglect within marriage?

Rebuilding myself began with small steps—reigniting old hobbies, reconnecting with friends, and seeking therapy. Each step helped me reclaim the person I had lost in the shadows of my marriage. Slowly, I started to recognise my worth beyond the confines of that relationship, embracing a renewed sense of self and purpose.

The Enemy Within

The internal forces that undermined my well-being and decision-making took control of my thoughts and overshadowed my emotional intelligence.

Fear became my biggest enemy, an invisible yet constant presence. It wasn't just a passing emotion, it was a force that took root deep in my soul, growing stronger with every moment of doubt and hesitation. It whispered in my ear, amplifying every insecurity, every worst-case scenario. I allowed it to paralyse me, to keep me trapped in a situation that no longer served me.

Even though I knew I deserved more, fear clung to me like a shadow, holding me back from stepping into the light of my own freedom. It was an enemy within, filling my mind with walls of 'what ifs' and 'shoulds,' keeping me trapped and away from the life I was meant to live.

Fear was not just a feeling but a cunning adversary lurking in the corners of my mind, waiting to strike whenever I dared to dream of freedom. My inner conflict created a battle, making it challenging to act despite knowing what needed to be done. Though I knew I had to leave, fear waged war inside me, turning every thought of escape into a nightmare of judgment and failure.

Fear held me back, keeping me stuck in situations that no longer brought me happiness. It confined me, stalling my growth and whispering that staying in my unhappiness was safer than facing the uncertainty of the unknown.

Fear often felt overwhelming, even though I had the power to overcome it. Its grip was suffocating, convincing me that freedom was a risk too great to take, even though deep down, I knew it was the only way forward.

From the beginning, fear was a constant companion, silently shaping every decision I made. It intensified as I faced the need for change and growth, keeping me paralysed in a state of inaction. As cracks in new relationships deepened, fear grew louder and more insistent, as if it knew its power over me was coming to an end.

Breaking free from fear was a turning point in my journey. Confronting it head-on was the hardest but most liberating step I had ever taken. The day I chose to walk away was the day I defeated my greatest enemy. Fear no longer had the final word in my life!

> *"Life is uncharted territory,*
> *It reveals its story one moment at a time."*
> **- Leo Buscaglia**

Uncharted Territory

It wasn't just my fears; self-abandonment also triggered a range of emotions and reactions within me. As I stepped into a new chapter of life, I found myself navigating uncharted territory without a clear map or direction. I had no choice but to embrace an optimistic outlook, seeing life through a lens of hope and possibility.

However, I found myself navigating uncharted territory after a breakdown, all while caring for four young children and welcoming a new member to the family—my first grandchild. It felt like embarking on a courageous expedition to the unknown carrying the responsibility of nurturing and protecting the precious journeys of those in my care.

These moments of exploration and hope became powerful tools, helping me transform challenging circumstances into opportunities for growth and resilience. They inspired me to face my "fear-venture" head-on, turning daunting trials into beacons of strength and hope woven into the tapestry of my new life story.

The uncertainty and adversity I faced were undoubtedly challenging and emotionally draining, but they also held the potential to foster growth and resilience. I had to be brave enough to embrace these experiences and the willingness to learn from them, growing stronger to face future challenges. By transforming these difficulties into new goals, I gained emotional strength and gradually evolved into a different, stronger version of myself—one step closer to becoming the best version of who I am.

As a result of my fear-venture, the uncharted territory I once feared turned into a journey of resilience, adaptability, and a renewed spirit of love for others. I realised I was evolving, discovering a vast and boundless landscape within my mind and heart.

The horizon is boundless in the territory of hope, glowing with the light of possibility. It is a place where no path is too steep, no obstacle is too great to overcome. The ground changes with every step—sometimes rough, sometimes smooth—but each turn brings a chance for renewal.

Here, doubts fade like morning mist, and resilience grows strong, rooted in belief. Hope becomes a steady guide, always shining, even in the darkest times. It calls you forward, toward a future not yet visible but full of promise and growth.

My dear reader and friends, the landscape of hope stretches endlessly, offering unseen paths that call you forward, even when you feel lost. Like a beacon of light in times of darkness, hope illuminates the way, guiding you through uncertainty and showing that there is always a way forward.

My self-abandonment

I remember creating a place of refuge within myself, a shelter where I could imagine a brighter tomorrow. My territory of hope became a sanctuary where I found solace in the belief that better days are waiting beyond the horizon.

As I nurtured this hope, it grew into something richer and more vibrant. Hope, I've learned, is like a garden—it flourishes with every act of faith. Its flowers bloom even in barren soil, always reaching for the light of a sun that never truly sets.

CHAPTER II

Emotional transformation against my unknown

The emotional transformation of my journey into the unknown was an inner evolution, where fear and uncertainty gave way to growth. Resilience and self-discovery began with anxiety and hesitation but gradually unfolded into courage and acceptance as I learned to face the unfamiliar with an open heart and mind.

At first, the unknown felt like a vast, shadowy expanse — a place where uncertainty weighed heavy, rooting itself in the pit of my stomach. My mind clung desperately to the safety of the familiar, resisting the pull of change. But as I continued forward, something within me began to shift. Each step into the unknown was met with quiet strength I didn't know I had.

With each stride, a small light grew brighter. The fear didn't disappear, but it no longer defined my journey. Instead, it fueled resilience, reminding me of my inner capacity. Transformation, I learned, is not about eliminating fear— it's about facing it and becoming more courageous, open, and alive.

At first, the unknown felt like an impenetrable wall. I resisted, unsure of what lay beyond. But slowly, I confronted it and realized the unknown is not an enemy— it's a doorway. The moment I accepted it, the fear lost its grip, and I began to move forward with curiosity instead of dread.

Emotional transformation against my unknown

Fear clings when we face the unknown, but as we push forward, it begins to soften. Every challenge reveals strength; every uncertainty becomes a lesson. The unknown, once a source of anxiety, turns into fertile ground for personal transformation.

From Paralysis to Possibility

The unknown often left me paralysed, freezing some of my decisions. But as I stepped into it, I realised that uncertainty opened doors to infinite possibilities. What was once felt like something to avoid became a space where I could create and grow, free from the limits of what I thought was possible.

This is my journey of discovery—not just of the external world, but of my inner self. Facing unfamiliar challenges uncovered new strengths, perspectives, and layers of who I am. In navigating the unknown, I transformed, becoming more resilient, adaptable, and aware of my true potential.

My New Map

Thus, the intrigue of a new chapter in my life opened the door to exploration and the risk of rewriting my story. It was a chance to reclaim my self-agency and redefine my sense of self and purpose in an authentic and empowering way. This process allowed me to find freedom from discomfort, stay present in my current narrative, and leave behind the weight of past life events.

I needed to trust myself to commence a new life chapter and focus on the outcomes I worked on. Therefore, to be accountable and responsible for my positive thinking and actions, I had to commit to living with positive thinking, a loving heart, giving service to people in need as well as showing compassion and respect for those who needed a friendly heart, a friendly hand, and a friendly shoulder to rest their heavy burdens. When I began showing or sharing my new personality with my friends, they laughed at me! "You are crazy!" Some of them expressed themselves.

I knew what I was doing and why I was transforming my persona. I knew with clear certainty that I needed to undergo an extraordinary transformation and personal growth within myself, as I couldn't survive anymore with the internal devastation nor be attracted to a pattern from the past. I had to win myself and uncover my new story and map.

On my new path, I encountered valuable challenges that taught me to live in harmony with myself, face adversity with strength, and foster profound self-discovery to nurture my inner core. Each life trajectory has submerged me in my consciousness and the world around me, and I enjoy life with abundance and inspiration to an emotionally straightforward and fulfilling journey.

However, my honesty didn't bring many friends into my circle, only the right ones. I learned to disregard what others may be thinking about me. The world only worries about themselves.

I also learned that people change; even my friends can become strangers. What did I love about the trajectory of my journey? Being with my own company, being happy, and not seeking company to fill the gap of my missing puzzle only debilitates my energy. I learned not to be afraid of being alone but to convert the fear into power. Therefore, my map taught me to become a priority and not an option.

Indeed, the magnetism within yourself develops with clarity, focused visualisation, and consistency to get what you focus on. On the other hand, if your thoughts are constantly negative, your inner energy will create a negative future! Then, why not allow ourselves to explore beyond the power of our minds/thoughts to receive the magic we await?

"Your choices reflect your priorities."
- Jean A. Stevens

CHAPTER III

The power against enmeshment

"Genuine inner freedom is the ultimate aim of life. It is the unspoken goal of every thought and action you take."
- David Simon

Salvador Minuchin (1974) used the term enmeshment to describe the unhealthy relationship dynamic often found within families, where personal boundaries are blurred or non-existent. In enmeshed relationships, the emotional boundaries between individuals are so entangled that personal identities, needs, and emotions become intertwined, leading to a lack of autonomy and individuality. This can manifest in several ways, including emotional over-involvement, control, and dependency.

When boundaries in a relationship are blurred, it's difficult to maintain a clear sense of identity within that dynamic. Therefore, the emotions and actions of one person often become tangled with those of others, said clinical psychologist Dr. John C Fox. In such enmeshed relationships, individuals may sacrifice their personal boundaries or lack them entirely.

After breaking free from the walls that had held me back in an unhealthy marriage, I met a man who seemed to offer the beginning of a new emotional journey. When I first met him, it felt like I had found someone who could finally meet my emotional needs. He knew how to make me feel special, seen, and understood. At first, it was everything I had been longing for—attention, love, and validation. But slowly, almost without realising it, I began to see the darker side of his charm. Little by little, I discovered his narcissism, hidden beneath the façade of the ideal partner. His words became manipulative, and his actions were more about control than love.

Still, I couldn't walk away. I had become so enmeshed in his web of lies that I didn't trust my own instincts anymore. He had convinced me that I needed him, that leaving would be a mistake, and I was afraid of failing in a relationship again. I was scared of what he might say, and I was scared of being alone. I stayed because I felt easier than facing the truth—that the person I believed could save me was the one destroying me.

I realised that I was living in an enmeshed relationship—a beautiful, decorated cage. From the outside, it seemed like I had constant attention, support, and care. But inside, I was suffocating. I was given everything I needed except the one thing that mattered most—internal freedom.

Every move I made was anticipated, every decision taken from me, as if I couldn't survive on my own. Despite the comfort I was promised, I felt a growing misery deep inside. I wasn't allowed to have boundaries or make my own choices, and with each passing day, I lost more of myself. I was trapped in a life where the needs of someone else overshadowed my identity, desires, and autonomy. The more he gave, the less I felt free.

I came to understand the painful contradiction between how my life appeared on the outside—'having everything'—and the internal reality of emotional confinement and the gradual loss of my true self.

Enmeshment or Dependency?

The nature of depending on a new relationship initially seemed to provide the emotional support and attention I longed for. I began to rely on my partner for validation and emotional fulfillment. His charm, attentiveness, and false sense of security made me feel safe, deepening my emotional attachment over time.

However, his subtle tactics of control gradually created a psychological dependency. I became increasingly reliant on his affection, and his influence reinforced my belief that I needed to stay. Like my previous relationship, where I felt emotionally neglected, this attachment filled a void, creating a strong bond that seemed comforting but ultimately eroded my autonomy.

I found myself trapped in a cycle of psychological dependency, believing my value came from him.

The more dependent I became, the more fearful I felt of leaving and feeling abandoned. I felt I was losing my emotional lifeline. Once again, I became stuck in a cycle of misery, blocked from growth by guilt, obligations, and the fear of social pressure and judgment.

What I truly wanted was to be strong enough to break free from this dependency and the self-enmeshment that kept me confined.

I want to emphasise that enmeshment is a term used in psychology to describe a dysfunctional relationship dynamic where personal boundaries are blurred or non-existent.

In a codependent relationship, one person relies on the other for self-worth while focusing on meeting the other person's needs. This dynamic often leads to resentment, anger, and an imbalance of effort in the relationship. The codependent person may even attempt to control their partner to meet their own emotional needs, perpetuating an unhealthy cycle.

CHAPTER IV

The silent war: Heart vs mind

Heart and mind—two powerful forces that often pull in opposite directions. The heart feels deeply, driven by emotional instincts, desires, and passion. Meanwhile, the mind is logical, rational, and attuned to societal norms. Together, they create what I call 'The Silent War.'

In this internal battle, emotions beat impulsively, demanding immediate action, while the mind remains calm and calculated, urging restraint.

In the quiet space between thoughts, war rages—unseen but felt. My heart pulses with reckless passion while my mind holds back with calm, calculated reasoning. Neither speaks loud, yet the conflict echoes through every decision, every hesitation.

Emotions have driven me to act impulsively, passionately, and without always considering the consequences.

"But did I follow my heart despite my mind's warning?" or " What if I am chasing the risk of pursuing happiness or clinging to emotional attachments?"

But my heart only justified its actions!

My heart, in its infinite yearning, speaks in pulses and beats. It doesn't understand reasoning, nor does it care. It craves connection, joy, and meaning, even when those come at the cost of peace. For my heart, every moment

The silent war: Heart vs mind

is an opportunity to feel alive, to follow passion, and to embrace the chaos of desire.

But in the silent war, my mind urges caution and practicality. I constantly weigh the pros and cons, considering long-term consequences and the acts of society's guardians. I try to prevent mistakes or heartbreak by being logical in emotional situations.

However, my consciousness believes it can protect me from pain, embarrassment, or failure. And, I am only a human, whose mind speaks in whispers of logic, trying to quiet the storm of emotions. It questions everything:

"Is this right?" or "Will this hurt?" and " What will they think?"

Throughout this chapter, I want to explore and share what binds us human beings—our emotional connections. Whether the love we give, the pain we endure, or the hope that keeps us moving forward, these bonds shape who we are. As I wave stories of joy, heartbreaker, and resilience, I also draw upon the timeless reflections of those who have delved into the profound depths of our shared human experience. From poets and philosophers to modern thinkers, these references remind us that we are never alone in our emotions and that through connection, we find meaning and strength.

Some notable author references – :

[Carl Jung- "The Archetypes and the Collective Unconscious"] Jung's work emphasizes the importance of connecting with the unconscious mind, where deeper aspects of the self are stored. He introduces the idea of individualisation, a process where one integrates the conscious and unconscious parts of the self for personal growth and wholeness.]

[Rumi (Sharon) Pearson- " The Essential Rumi" The Sufi mystic Rumi often wrote about the connection between the self and the divine within, expressing a deep sense of inner awareness and love that transcends the external world.]

[Thich Nhat Hanh- "The Miracle of Mindfulness" A Vietnamese Buddhist monk, Hanh speaks extensively about cultivating mindfulness and conscious awareness to connect deeply with oneself, leading to inner peace and compassion for others.]

The cost of the conflict between my heart and mind led to emotional paralysis and fatigue. My emotional weight was a war of self-perception, lack of peace, and the conflict of understanding what I, as an individual, genuinely want.

The silent war: Heart vs mind

Therefore, I can illustrate that when a human being gets caught between their heart and mind, their soul may feel fractured, each step towards passion may be met with a whisper of doubt, and every rational decision may leave an emptiness where joy could have bloomed. In this silent war, there are no victors—only casualties of indecision.

Thus, the heart and mind were never meant to be enemies. One needs the other. Passion without direction burns out; logic without feeling becomes lifeless. Perhaps the proper path forward is not to silence one but to hear them both—to let the heart dream and the mind build, to follow emotions, and yet guide them with reason.

I acknowledge that balancing our emotional beings throughout the central heart and mind human body parts is not easily maintained, and the war between heart and mind never truly ends. However, we can become stronger and more self-aware by learning to navigate this inner conflict with awareness. That silent war becomes less about defeating one side and more about understanding both.

Also, the war between heart and mind is never truly won, but we can discover who we are through the battle. In every choice, we decide which voice to follow, knowing that reasons or emotions and the delicate dance between them shape our journey.

The emotional push and pull between the heart and the mind

1. The Pull of Love vs. the Push of Logic

Scenario: A character is deeply in love with someone, but the relationship is complicated and frowned upon by society. Their heart pulls them toward the connection, urging them to embrace the love they feel, while their mind weighs the risks and consequences, reminding them of the potential fallout.

Heart's Voice:

"Every moment with them feels like I'm finally breathing like I'm truly alive. What does it matter what the world thinks? This is love—how can it be wrong? I can't imagine my life without them. What is logic in the face of this feeling, this joy that floods my soul every time I see them?"

Mind's Voice:

"But think about it—what if this all falls apart? What about your family, your reputation? They're not right for you, and deep down, you know it. The odds are against you. Love doesn't pay the bills, and it doesn't erase the consequences. Are you ready to throw your life into chaos for something that may not last?"

Engagement:

We've all likely felt the emotional pull of the heart—its deep yearning and urgency—while also hearing the cold, rational voice of the mind. This inner conflict creates a tension many can relate to, especially if they've faced similar dilemmas.

2. The Desire for Freedom vs. Fear of the Unknown

Scenario: A character feels trapped in a secure but unfulfilling job and dreams of leaving it behind to follow their passion. Their heart urges them to take the leap, chasing the dream that fills them with excitement and purpose. But their mind pulls them back, clinging to the safety and stability of their current life, warning of the uncertainty and risks that lie ahead.

Heart's Voice:

"You've always wanted this—this is your chance to live the life you've dreamed of finally. Think of the joy, the freedom, the fulfillment! Staying here, in this cage, it's killing your spirit. You deserve more, and you know it. Don't waste another second—go before it's too late!"

Mind's Voice:

"But what if it doesn't work out? What if you fail and lose everything? You have security here—why risk it all for some uncertain future? People count on you. You can't just walk away from responsibilities. Be sensible; keep what you have. Dreams are nice, but reality pays the bills."

Engagement:

We've likely felt the excitement and longing for freedom that the heart desires, while also grappling with the fear and doubt that the mind raises. This inner conflict is deeply relatable, drawing us into the character's struggle and making us emotionally invested in their decision.

3. Holding On vs. Letting Go

Scenario: A character is in a relationship that no longer makes them happy, but they can't bring themselves to leave. Their heart clings to the emotional bond, memories, and comfort while their mind urges them to break free.

Heart's Voice:

"But remember the good times? Remember when you were happy, how they held you, how they made you laugh?

There's still love there; it's just buried. Maybe things will change. You've invested so much time and energy—don't give up now. Isn't this worth fighting for? Isn't love about enduring the hard times?"

Mind's Voice:

"But how long will you keep waiting? Things haven't changed in years. You deserve more than just memories of happiness—you deserve to be happy now. You're holding onto a version of them that doesn't exist anymore. Isn't it time to let go and move on? Staying here is only hurting you both."

Engagement:

Many of us may resonate with this push-and-pull between holding onto the past and facing the truth of the present. The heart's hope and nostalgia clash with the mind's need for closure and growth, creating emotional tension that draws us in.

4. The Risk of Vulnerability vs. the Safety of Silence

Scenario: A character has the opportunity to confess their feelings to someone they care about but is afraid of rejection. The heart wants to be open and vulnerable, while the mind fears the consequences of exposure.

Heart's Voice:

"Tell them. Tell them now, before it's too late. What if they feel the same? You'll never know if you don't try. What's the point of hiding how you feel? You've been waiting for this moment—don't let fear take it from you. Vulnerability is the only way to real connection."

Mind's Voice:

"But what if they don't feel the same? What if you ruin everything? Right now, things are good—why risk the awkwardness, the rejection, the pain? You could lose the friendship, the comfort of what you have. Isn't it safer to stay quiet? It's not worth the risk."

Engagement:

We've all likely experienced the intense internal battle between the desire for emotional openness and the fear of rejection. This conflict is universally relatable, touching on the vulnerability we feel when we risk putting our hearts on the line.

5. Forgiveness vs. Protecting Oneself

Scenario: A character has been deeply hurt by someone they love. Their heart wants to forgive and move forward, but their mind reminds them of the hurt and warns against trusting again too easily.

Heart's Voice:

"They're sorry, and you know they didn't mean to hurt you. You've been through so much together—don't throw it all away over one mistake. Forgiveness could bring peace, and you can't keep carrying this bitterness forever. Your love is stronger than this."

Mind's Voice:

"But look at what they did. Can you really trust them again? What if they hurt you again? You have to protect yourself—self-preservation comes first. Forgiveness is not the same as forgetting, and you can't just pretend like nothing happened. Is it worth the risk?"

Engagement:

Here, the emotional pull of forgiveness and the desire for healing clash with the rational need for self-protection. We feel the vulnerability of letting go of hurt, even as the mind urges caution and self-preservation.

These examples highlight the push-pull dynamic between heart and mind in emotionally charged situations. Each scenario invites us to step into the character's shoes, experience their internal conflict, and connect it to our own struggles, fostering a deep emotional connection.

CHAPTER V

Causality or Reality

Was it causality or reality that brought me to you, only to plunge me into a profound emotional pain?

The encounter felt preordained, yet the consequences were too real, a stark reminder of a life that did not truly belong to me.

In the depth of the pain, I confronted the harsh truth that I had allowed my identity to be woven into the fabric of someone else's needs and desires.

It was a painful awakening to realise that I had sacrificed parts of myself for a connection that left me feeling hollow.

Through the agony of this experience, I learned that sometimes the most profound lessons emerge from our deepest wounds.

This journey was not simply a series of unfortunate events but rather an opportunity for transformation, a chance to reclaim my autonomy and redefine what it means to live a life that truly reflects who I am.

The tension between experiencing emotional pain and reclaiming self-identity is profound. It is a confrontation with the consequences of living a life concealed beneath a mask. In the depths of that anguish, I began to recognise how I had surrendered my identity. The suffering became a mirror, reflecting the parts of myself I had buried in pursuit of what I believed love should be.

What once felt like an intoxicating connection slowly revealed its true nature—a cage of dependency that stifled my spirit and silenced my voice.

By recognising the power of thought, I was able to turn causality into a driving force for my personal growth.

As I began to realise the profound impact that my thoughts had on my reality, it became clear that they were more than fleeting ideas—they were the seeds of my emotional state. Every thought carried the potential to shape my experience, influencing my emotions and actions in ways I hadn't fully grasped before.

Understanding this connection between thought and outcome became a turning point, empowering my desire for emotional growth.

By consciously choosing thoughts that aligned with the person I wanted to become, I started reclaiming control over my emotional landscape, transforming how I faced challenges and embraced healing."

The capacity to heal the heart is found in the trust of your conscious living, bringing peace to a wounded soul.
- Bethsaida Hingston

CHAPTER VI

Fear of self-reclamation

Personal reclamation is an empowering journey of rediscovering and reclaiming your true self after periods of loss, emotional turmoil, or the weight of societal expectations. It's a deliberate choice to rise above the circumstances that once confined you and to fully embrace the authenticity of your own identity, values, and desires.

Recognising What's Been Lost

The first step in personal reclamation is acknowledging what has been lost, whether it's your sense of self, autonomy, or even your emotional voice.

This could stem from toxic relationships, societal pressures, or life's hardships that led you away from your core identity. Often, this recognition involves moments of vulnerability, where you face external challenges and your own internal fears.

Forging a New Path

Personal reclamation is about breaking free from the past and forging a new path guided by your terms and conditions.

This means setting emotional boundaries, redefining relationships, and creating a life that aligns with your true self. It requires courage to embrace change and a willingness to move through discomfort.

Healing and Rebuilding Trust

An essential part of this journey is healing, which involves forgiving yourself for past mistakes and nurturing self-compassion.

Reclaiming trust in yourself is essential—believing in your strength to face life's challenges, your wisdom to make better decisions, and your resilience to recover from setbacks. This is where self-trust begins to grow, as you learn to depend on your own inner guidance.

Freedom and Ownership

At the heart of personal reclamation is the experience of freedom—the freedom to live authentically without needing approval or validation from others.

This journey gives you the space to honour your own needs, passions, and aspirations, empowering you to live fully and unapologetically.

Ultimately, personal reclamation is a powerful act of self-liberation, where you reclaim your narrative, live with intention, and own every aspect of your journey. It's about moving beyond survival to truly thrive, embracing every part of who you are, and finding strength in your story.

Dear Reader,

Every journey of self-reclamation begins with an encounter with fear. We may not always recognise it at first, but fear lurks in the corners of our minds, holding us back from stepping into our true power.

It tells us to stay in familiar, safe places—even if those places are confining or unfulfilling. It whispers doubts about whether we are worthy of change, capable of transformation, or strong enough to face the unknown.

For me, fear took the form of resistance—resistance to change, resistance to facing the truth about what I needed to let go of, and even resistance to admitting that I deserved something better.

I feared what life would look like if I broke free from the expectations and roles I had been playing for so long. The fear of losing what was familiar often outweighed the desire for freedom.

But I came to realise that fear is part of the process. It's a natural response to stepping into the unknown, to leaving behind the safety of what we've always known—even if that 'safety' is suffocating.

Self-reclamation requires us to confront those fears, to sit with them, and to understand that they do not define us. They are merely signposts on the road to growth, guiding us toward the parts of ourselves that need healing, attention, and ultimately, release.

Through this journey, I learned that courage isn't the absence of fear—it's moving forward in spite of it. Each step, no matter how small, became an act of reclaiming my power. I invite you to reflect on your own fears and how they might be holding you back. What are the stories you've been telling yourself? What would happen if you decided to rewrite them?

Understanding Your Fears

What would the language of fear sound like?

1. **Fear of abandonment:** Individuals in enmeshed relationships may fear that breaking through the enmeshment could lead to abandonment. This fear is often rooted in past experiences of abandonment or rejection, and individuals may feel that maintaining the enmeshed dynamic is the only way they can avoid being alone.

2. **Loss of Identity:** Enmeshed individuals may have a deep-seated fear of losing their sense of self if they were to establish healthier boundaries. They may have become so intertwined with the other person that they struggle to differentiate their thoughts, feelings, and desires from those of the other person. Breaking free from enmeshment means confronting the loss of identity and taking on the challenge of rediscovering yourself.

3. **Guilt and Obligation:** Enmeshed individuals may feel guilt when considering breaking through the enmeshment. They may believe that setting boundaries or pursuing their interests could be selfish or hurtful to the other person. Feelings of obligation and a desire to please others can make it difficult for individuals to prioritize their well-being.

4. **Fear of Confrontation:** Confronting the dynamics of an enmeshed relationship and setting boundaries can be emotionally challenging. Individuals may also fear the potential conflict, backlash, or emotional turmoil from asserting their independence and autonomy. This fear of independence can lead to avoidance of necessary conversations and actions.

5. **Lack of Autonomy:** Enmeshed individuals may have grown accustomed to relying on the other person for emotional support, decision-making, and identity validation. The prospect of breaking through enmeshment may trigger anxiety about assuming full responsibility for their well-being and choices, which can feel overwhelming and unfamiliar.

6. **Uncertainty and Change:** Breaking through enmeshment often involves stepping into the unknown and embracing change. Individuals may fear the uncertainty of life outside the enmeshment dynamics and the potential discomfort associated with establishing new, healthier relationships.

Enmeshed Fear

My journey of self-reclamation began in the depths of enmeshed fear—a suffocating weight that made escape feel impossible, leaving me with the darkest thought of not existing at all. In moments of despair, I felt trapped in a laybirth with no way out. Each turn led me deeper into the shadows, obscuring any hope glimmer.

Yet, within that darkness, I found a flicker of possibility—the unknown stood before me, not as an abyss but as an invitation to begin again. The vision of a new motherhood began to unfold, one where I could break free from the chains of my past and embrace the strength necessary to keep going.

As I sat with my dear and loving friend, Robyn, drawing strength from her resilience and wisdom, I began to understand that the path ahead, while uncertain, held the promise of renewal. In those quiet moments of reflection, I found the courage to imagine a future filled with love and purpose. Cradling the new life that would emerge from my arms.

This vision of new life wrapped around me like a warm embrace, igniting a flame of hope against the shadows of despair. I imagined cradling the child who would embody not just a new beginning but a testament to my journey of survival. It was a promise that I could create a life defined by love, nurturing, and the strength of my own spirit.

This transformative journey is not a straight path but a series of brave steps taken despite fear. With each moment of vulnerability, I uncovered the strength of resilience and began to rediscover my identity beyond the limits of my past. I wasn't merely surviving—I was choosing to fully embrace life, holding this new chapter in my arms with fierce determination to nurture and protect it.

I stepped into a new chapter, one of the most transformative journeys of my life. It was a path shaped by the complexity of fear, the struggle of self-reclamation, and the hope that comes with the prospect of a new life through motherhood.

I knew it was time to act—to set emotional boundaries, embrace self-forgiveness, and reclaim my power—marking a transformative step in my emotional growth.

Emotional Boundaries

It became clear to me that without emotional boundaries, I was not only letting others drain my energy but also keeping myself trapped in cycles of guilt and self-blame. I came to see that I had been giving so much to others while neglecting to forgive myself.

Setting boundaries wasn't about shutting people out—it was about creating a sanctuary within myself where I could heal, reflect, and grow.

By learning to protect my emotional energy, I allowed myself to forgive my past mistakes and begin the journey of self-reclamation. In those moments of quiet, behind the boundaries I had set, I found the clarity and strength I needed to reconnect with who I truly am.

Remi Pearson, founder of The Coaching Institute, talks extensively about emotional boundaries and personal growth. She emphasizes that setting healthy emotional boundaries is crucial for self-care and self-reclamation.

These boundaries help to define the limits of how others' behaviours and emotions impact you, empowering you to take control of your emotional well-being.

Pearson's model focuses on authenticity and autonomy, using boundaries to maintain integrity in relationships and interactions. By setting these boundaries, it fosters emotional freedom, helps avoid becoming entangled in others' expectations or societal pressures, and promotes personal empowerment.

The Power of Emotional Boundaries

Protecting yourself while staying connected:

Emotional boundaries are the invisible lines we draw to protect our inner world—our thoughts, feelings, and emotional energy. They define where we end and where others begin, allowing us to engage in relationships without losing our sense of self. While often overlooked, emotional boundaries are essential for healthy, balanced interactions with others.

Why Do Emotional Boundaries Matter?

Without boundaries, we risk being overwhelmed by others' emotions or losing ourselves in their needs and expectations. Boundaries serve as a form of emotional self-defense, helping us avoid enmeshment and emotional burnout. They allow us to show empathy and care for others without sacrificing our own mental and emotional well-being.

However, setting emotional boundaries doesn't mean closing yourself off. It's not about shutting people out or being distant—it's about creating a space where both your needs and theirs can coexist. Healthy boundaries let you love deeply and wisely.

Signs of Poor Emotional Boundaries

When emotional boundaries are blurred or nonexistent, it can lead to:

Emotional exhaustion: Constantly absorbing other people's emotions can leave you feeling drained and disconnected from your own feelings.

People-pleasing: The fear of rejection or conflict may lead you to prioritize others' needs over your own, causing resentment and burnout.

Loss of identity: Without boundaries, you may lose sight of who you are and what you want, as your sense of self becomes too entangled with others.

How to Establish and Maintain Emotional Boundaries

Establishing emotional boundaries requires self-awareness and the courage to communicate your needs clearly.

Steps to creating emotional boundaries:

1. **Identify your emotional limits:** Take time to reflect on what makes you feel uncomfortable, drained, or overwhelmed in relationships. These feelings are often signals that your boundaries are being crossed.
2. **Practice saying no:** It can be difficult, but it is critical to learn to say no when something feels emotionally draining or unhealthy. Remember that saying no doesn't make you selfish—it makes you honest about your capacity.
3. **Communicate openly and respectfully:** Once you're clear on your boundaries, express them calmly and directly to others. For example, "I need some time to process my emotions before I can talk about this" sets a clear boundary without alienating the other person.

4. **Be consistent:** Emotional boundaries require maintenance. Setting a boundary but letting it slide over time can send mixed signals. Be consistent in upholding your boundaries, even if it feels uncomfortable at first.

The Emotional Growth That Follows

Learning to set emotional boundaries is an act of self-respect and emotional growth. It allows you to reclaim your emotional space and invites more balanced, fulfilling relationships.

By setting boundaries, you show others how to treat you and empower yourself to live authentically without being overwhelmed by external emotional demands.

In time, emotional boundaries become the foundation for deeper, healthier connections—ones built on mutual respect and understanding rather than emotional overextension.

As I look back on my journey of learning to set emotional boundaries, I see how pivotal it was in transforming not only my relationships with others but also my relationship with myself.

At first, I resisted, believing that boundaries would create distance between me and the people I loved. But I soon discovered the opposite—they became the foundation for deeper, more authentic connections.

This experience taught me that boundaries aren't walls but bridges to healthier emotional spaces. By recognizing my limits, I created room for healing and the emotional growth I had been seeking.

CHAPTER VII

Echoes of the frozen summit

The echoes of isolation, introspection, and the journey toward self-reclamation have a profound and solitary accent.

The echoes of past experiences and the quest to discover one's true self amidst challenging circumstances.

Standing atop the frozen summit, the world stretched out in a silent expanse beneath me. The biting cold was a stark contrast to the warmth I once felt within, now replaced by a chill of isolation and introspection.

Each breath I took was a reminder of the journey I had undertaken—one filled with echoes of past pain and the quiet whispers of a heart longing to rediscover its true rhythm. Here, amidst the icy peaks, I faced the echos of my former self, seeking clarity and the courage to embrace a new beginning.

Isolation stripped away the distraction of everyday life, leaving only the raw truth of my existence. In the stillness, I could hear the echoes of my past, each memory a crystallised moment that had shaped who I was. This solitude was both daunting and liberating, offering a chance to sift through the layers of dependency and enmeshment that had clouded my sense of self.

Overcoming Challenges

The accent to the summit was fraught with challenges, mirroring the internal battles I faced. Each icy gust felt like a reminder of the emotional turmoil I had endured. But reaching the top was more than survival—it was triumph, proof that I possessed the strength to overcome obstacles that once seemed insurmountable.

Challenges, born from adversity and shadowed by discomfort, can become our most vulnerable yet valuable tools for self-reclamation.

Nevertheless, discomfort and inadequacy can weigh heavily on our souls, making us doubt our worth. And yet, let me tell you something: you are more capable and resilient than you realise.

You Are Better Than You Think You Are!

Yes, You Are!

Reflecting on how past experiences and memories shape present emotions and decisions is like hearing echoes reverberate through the mountains. The echoes around the summit weren't just sounds—they were fragments of the past, resonating through the corridors of my mind. They reminded me of moments of joy and pain, connections lost, and identities sacrificed. Understanding these echoes was a crucial step in my journey toward healing, allowing me to piece together the fragments of my true self that had been scattered by so many years of emotional entanglement.

I clearly remember the first time I felt truly alone—standing in a crowd yet feeling invisible. It was like being stranded on a frozen peak, surrounded by beauty but consumed by cold isolation. It was during this moment that I realised the extent of my dependency and the urgent need to reclaim my identity. The summit symbolised my resilience, a place where I could confront and overcome my fears, which were the obstacles holding me back.

Emotional Journey

The journey to the frozen summit was more than just physical climb—it was an emotional odyssey. At the base, I was burdened by dependence and fear, each step forward a struggle against the weight of past life events. As I climbed higher, the air grew thinner, symbolising the shedding of old layers and the emergence of a more authentic self.

By the time I reached the summit, the echoes of my former life had transformed into a harmonious melody of self-awareness and a future defined by my own terms.

Echoes on the frozen summit can serve as a powerful metaphor for the struggles and triumphs of personal transformation. It reminds us that we hold the power to create life chapters that resonate deeply within us, shaping a future rooted in our true selves.

Have You Felt Broken?

Are You Perfect?

Perfection is an illusion we often chase, driven by societal expectations or the desire to fit a particular mold. Yet, to be human is to embrace imperfection. The question, "Are you perfect?" invites us to reflect on this impossible standard, while the more profound question, "Have you felt broken?" speaks to the heart of our shared human experience.

Most of us have felt broken at some point—whether through relationships, loss, personal failures, or circumstances beyond our control. Yet, brokenness doesn't signify the end; it's a temporary state, a fracture in the journey. In fact, those moments of brokenness often hold the most potential for growth and healing.

The Japanese art of Kintsugi, where broken pottery is repaired with gold, symbolizes beautifully that what was once broken is now more valuable and beautiful for having been healed.

When you have been asked, "Are you perfect?" How did you respond? It's a question that can feel unsettling. Many of us feel internal pressure to live up to unrealistic ideals of perfection—whether in our appearance, relationships, careers or even how we manage emotions. Perfection suggests flawlessness, an unachievable standard that often leaves us feeling inadequate in its wake.

But what if perfection isn't the goal? What if the very essence of being human lies in our imperfection? The cracks in our character, the scars of our experiences—these are not things to hide but elements that shape our uniqueness and depth. Our imperfections make us real, relatable, and resilient.

Who is perfect in this world? I am not perfect! Are you?

- Have you ever felt that striving for perfection has disconnected you from your authentic self?
- When you have felt broken, what did that moment reveal about who you are or what you need?
- How have your imperfections allowed you to grow in ways perfection never could?
- What would life look like if you embraced your brokenness and imperfections as integral parts of your journey?

Through this reflection, I invite you to look inward and acknowledge your own struggles and the beauty in your imperfections. Brokenness is not failure, and imperfection is not weakness. Both are part of what makes us human, resilient, and capable of profound transformation.

Steps to Self-Reclamation

Each step is designed to guide you in rediscovering and reclaiming your true self:

1. **Self-Reflection**: Take time to reflect on your experiences, values, and what has led you to feel disconnected from yourself. This could involve journaling, meditation, or even discussing your thoughts with a trusted friend or therapist. Understanding your past can provide insights into your present feelings and guide your journey forward.

2. **Establishing Boundaries:** Setting clear emotional boundaries is vital. This means identifying what is acceptable in your relationships and what is not. Learning to say no and prioritising your needs can protect your emotional well-being and create space for growth.
3. **Seeking Support:** Surround yourself with a supportive network of friends, family, or professionals who understand your journey. Support groups or therapy can offer a safe environment for sharing experiences and gaining encouragement from those who have faced similar challenges.
4. **Practicing Self-Compassion:** Treat yourself with kindness and understanding, especially when confronting difficult emotions or past mistakes. Self-compassion fosters resilience and helps you accept yourself without harsh judgment.
5. **Setting Goals:** Define small, achievable goals that align with your values and aspirations. Breaking your reclamation process into manageable steps can boost motivation and provide a sense of accomplishment as you progress.
6. **Embracing Vulnerability:** Allow yourself to be vulnerable by expressing your emotions and needs. This can deepen your connections with others and help you reclaim parts of yourself that may have been suppressed.
7. **Engaging in Mindfulness:** Mindfulness practices, such as meditation or yoga, can help ground you

in the present moment and reduce anxiety. Being mindful allows you to observe your thoughts and feelings without judgment, facilitating a clearer understanding of yourself.
8. **Celebrating Progress:** Acknowledge and celebrate your achievements, no matter how small. Recognising your progress reinforces positive change and motivates you to continue on your path to self-reclamation.

No One is Allowed to Misjudge You

In life, we often meet people who misjudge us—people who form opinions without understanding our whole story and instead, reduce us to a moment, mistake, or assumption. But here is the truth worth holding onto: no one is allowed to define you but you!

Their judgments are not reflections of your worth. They are projections of their own limitations. You are a complex, evolving being on a unique journey that no one else can fully comprehend. Your truth is yours to own, and no one's misjudgment can strip away the value of your experiences.

Life is our greatest gift—a continuous journey of learning, growing, and progressing. So why not extend mercy and compassion to ourselves? What stops us from embracing our humanity?

There's profound comfort in accepting that we are imperfect beings. When we acknowledge our imperfections, they become tools for understanding who we are and who we want to become. Imperfection isn't a flaw; it's a guide, shaping us into our truest selves.

> *"Reclaiming yourself is the joy of your tears rolling down as you leave all behind and climb back up to the restoration of your true self."*
> **– Bethsaida Hingston**

My dear friend, being judgemental in my literature is not allowed!

Instead, I want to offer you a heartfelt message: this journey of transformation is one of love and acceptance. Embrace it with kindness and forgiveness, as it leads to self-reclamation and a new life filled with pure intentions. This is a path to honouring your values, believing in yourself, and building trust within.

Recognising the loss of self can be a powerful turning point—a chance to reflect on how we've become disconnected from our true selves. This self-alienation often stems from societal expectations, trauma, poor decisions, or unconscious behaviors. Yet, acknowledging this disconnection is the first step toward finding our way back and reclaiming who we truly are.

Leaving the past behind opens up a number of opportunities for personal growth and emotional well-being.

Benefits when leaving the past behind:

1. **Improved Mental Health:** Letting go of past grievances can significantly enhance your mental health. It allows you to move away from negative emotions like guilt, regret, and sadness, leading to a more positive outlook on life.
2. **Increased Happiness:** By releasing the burdens of the past, you can create space for joy and fulfillment in the present. This shift helps you focus on what truly matters and appreciate your circumstances.
3. **New Possibilities:** Letting go makes room for new experiences and opportunities. Just like cleaning out a cluttered closet can help you discover things you forgot you had, moving on from past events allows you to embrace new paths and adventures that can enrich your life.
4. **Self-Discovery and Growth:** The process of leaving the past behind often leads to greater self-awareness and personal growth. It encourages you to reassess your beliefs and values, allowing you to redefine your identity and purpose.
5. **Empowerment:** By acknowledging that the past does not define you, you regain control over

your life. This empowerment can help you build confidence in your decisions and aspirations.

6. **Stronger Relationships:** Letting go of past grievances can also improve your relationships. Reducing resentment and enabling you to connect with others more genuinely allows for healthier dynamics.

Overall, moving on is crucial for embracing life fully and can catalyse new beginnings.

*"If you feel you are broken,
please know you can be mended."*
- Jeffrey R. Holland

CHAPTER VIII

My consciousness after a journey of healing

Emerging from the depths of my healing journey, I feel as though my consciousness has profoundly transformed. It's as if I have awoken from a long, disorienting dream where shadows obscured my true self's light. The path to healing is rarely linear; it is a tapestry woven with threads of pain, resilience, self-discovery, and, ultimately, liberation.

In my quiet moments of reflection, I have come to understand the layers of my identity. I am no longer defined by my past wounds or the narratives others imposed upon me. My consciousness is now a space where I embrace my strengths and vulnerabilities. I recognise that every scar tells a story of survival and growth, each a testament to my resilience.

Reclaiming My Voice

Through healing, I have reclaimed my voice, once stifled by fear and doubt. My thoughts and feelings no longer hide in the shadows; they rise to the surface, demanding acknowledgment. I've learned to express myself authentically, allowing my truth to resonate. Speaking up has become an act of self-love, a declaration that I am worthy of being heard and understood.

Letting Go of Judgement

With this newfound awareness comes a liberation from self-judgement. The harsh critic within me, once relentless and unforgiving, has softened. I understand that imperfection is not a flaw but an essential part of being human. I have learned to show myself compassion, embracing mistakes and missteps without letting them define my worth. Letting go of judgment has opened the door to more profound self-acceptance.

Embracing the Present

My consciousness now resides in the present moment. The chains of the past no longer bind me, and I refuse to let fear of the future dictate my happiness. I embrace each day as an opportunity for growth, joy, and connection. I find beauty in the ordinary, reveling in the simple moments that once felt mundane. Each breath I take is a reminder of the life I am actively choosing to live.

Connection with Others

Healing has also reshaped my relationships. I approach connections with a sense of authenticity. I seek out those who uplift and inspire me. I recognise the value of supportive relationships that honour my journey. My consciousness has expanded to embrace empathy, allowing me to see others through a lens of understanding and compassion. In sharing my story, I create space for others to share theirs, fostering a community of healing and growth.

Hope for the Future

As I look forward, I carry the lessons I have learned along the way. My consciousness is filled with hope—a belief in my ability to navigate whatever challenges come my way. I understand that I will continue to grow and evolve as life unfolds. With each step, I nurture a sense of purpose, commit to caring for my spirit, and embrace the fullness of life.

Reflecting on my consciousness after this healing journey, I know that I am not merely surviving—I am thriving. I have emerged not just as a survivor of my past but as an empowered individual ready to embrace the beauty of the present and the promise of the future.

The secret of health for both
mind and body are not to mourn for the past,
worry about the future, or anticipate troubles ….
But to live in the present moment
Wislely and eaenestly.
- Buddha

Signs of Self-loss

Self-loss can manifest as a deep sense of dissatisfaction, feeling trapped in a life that we didn't choose, or the recognition that our decisions are not aligned with our authentic values. When we live based on external approval, habitual patterns, or unconscious drives, we gradually lose sight of our desires and potential.

Self-reclamation often starts with an awakening—when we realise we have been living on autopilot, guided by unconscious forces or external influences. Breaking free from past conditioning can be challenging, as self-reclamation involves identifying and reconstructing the inner beliefs that shape our behaviour. Carl Jung referred to this as integrating the "shadow," the part of ourselves that represses or denies, often driving unconscious behaviour. Therefore, reclaiming the self means bringing hidden aspects into the light.

By creating new, healthier patterns that have kept us stuck, we have become conscious, consequently welcoming authentic self-transformation despite the difficult moments that we have experienced.

Healing and Forgiveness

Reclaiming myself often meant healing from past mistakes or regrets. My healing process involved forgiveness. The principal forgiveness I had to practice was learning to forgive myself with self-compassion. However, my past decisions and facing the truth of the pain brought guilt, shame, and regret, especially when I realised that I had hurt others along the way.

Shedding my past self required learning to let go of what once gave me a sense of security and belonging. When I finally let go, I felt a significant loss. This letting go led to an identity crisis, leaving me unsure of who I was in my own narrative. The vulnerability of trying to reclaim myself felt like confronting a shadow, forcing me to face aspects of my personality that I had begun to deny out of social discomfort.

Self-reclamation, for me, became an act of radical honesty. It left me exposed and vulnerable, requiring me to confront my weaknesses and emotionally painful fears.

While self-reclamation can be painful, this pain is often a necessary part of the transformation process. It represents the breaking down of old, limiting structures and the emergence of something more authentic.

The pain of self-reclamation is not without purpose. It catalyses deep healing, personal freedom, and the rediscovery of one's true self. By leaning into the discomfort, we open the doors to greater self-awareness, fulfillment, and autonomy.

My consciousness after a journey of healing

Loss and Scars in a Narrative

Loss can be a defining moment in anyone's life, much like a scar that marks a profound change. The pain of loss might never fully disappear, but like a scar, it's something we learn to live with, carrying its lessons and wisdom forward. Whether it's the loss of a loved one, a dream, or an identity, loss leaves its mark. These marks, however, are proof that we have survived, healed, and continue to rise.

The concept of a scar in the story of survival carries deep symbolic meaning. Scars represent the visible and invisible marks left on a person after enduring difficult experiences, struggles, or trauma.

They are the reminders of what has been survived, the healing that followed, and the strength gained through the process. Here's how you can frame scars within the narrative of survival.

1. The Scar as a Symbol of Strength

"My scars are not just marks on my skin—they are symbols of resilience, reminders that I have survived what was meant to break me."

Scars show that you've endured hardship and lived through it. They are a testimony to your strength, showing that despite pain and difficulty, you've made it through to the other side.

2. Scars Tell a Story of Growth

"Each scar tells a story, a chapter of pain and triumph, and a testament to my growth. These marks are not signs of weakness but of wisdom gained through experience."

Survival often means change—whether emotional, physical, or spiritual. Scars represent this evolution, showing how you've transformed from one version of yourself to another through the challenges you faced.

3. Healing Beyond the Scar

"The scar may remain, but the wound is healed. My survival is not defined by what hurt me, but by how I chose to heal and move forward."

Healing doesn't mean forgetting or erasing the past. It means learning to live with it, growing from it, and becoming stronger as a result. Scars show the healing process is complete, though the memories may remain.

4. The Scar as a Reminder of Courage

"Every scar on my body is a medal of courage, a reminder that I fought to stay whole, even when the world tried to tear me apart."

Scars can serve as a badge of honour. They reflect moments where you faced fear, uncertainty, or pain, but still found the courage to keep going. They tell the world that you didn't give up.

5. Scars as Proof of Survival

"My scars are the proof of my survival. They carry the echoes of my journey, from struggle to strength, from despair to hope."

Survival is about more than just making it through; it's about thriving despite the odds. Scars are the evidence that you've overcome, and they are proof of your resilience.

6. Scars as a Sign of Transformation

"Scars are not the end of my story; they are the beginning of a new chapter. Each scar represents a battle fought, and each victory shapes me into who I am becoming."

Survival doesn't just mean enduring; it's about transformation. Scars reflect the changes you've undergone and the person you've become because of your experiences.

7. The Invisible Scars

"Not all scars are visible; some are etched deeply within my soul. They may not be seen by others, but they shape the way I live and love."

While physical scars are visible, many people carry emotional scars that are invisible to the outside world. These scars, though unseen, are just as powerful in shaping one's life and journey.

8. Scars as a Source of Empathy

"I wear my scars not as burdens, but as bridges to connect with others who have known pain. My scars give me the ability to understand, to empathise, and to offer support."

When you've been through hardship, you gain a unique understanding of others who are suffering. Your scars allow you to empathise with others and offer a hand to lift them up.

My consciousness after a journey of healing

In conclusion, the scars of a survivor are like pages in a book—their stories often untold but always significant. Each scar, whether physical or emotional, serves as a reminder of a moment when life tried to rupture you. But instead of shattering, you healed.

These scars are the marks of a survivor, imprints of courage and resilience, the silent witnesses to your strength. They are not flaws, but proof that you faced the storms and emerged on the other side, perhaps scarred, but forever transformed.

CHAPTER IX

Uncertainty as a mask

My dear reader,

As I navigate the intricate landscapes of my thoughts and the environments that surround me, I often find myself becoming an observer—not just of the world around me, but also of my own inner dialogues.

There were moments when I felt as if I was watching a game unfold, each character representing facets of my experiences, emotions, and the relationships I held dear. Through this lens, I began understanding the subtle interplay of feelings and actions that shaped my life's realities.

I invite you to journey with me as I share snippets of this narrative. Imagine the scenes where light meets shadow, hope dances with fear, and the whispers of the past gently echo in the present. This exploration is not merely about recounting events; it's about the reflections that arise from the individual and the wisdom they impart.

Together, let's unravel these stories, discovering the threads that connect us all in our quest for understanding and emotional growth.

The uncertainty can act like a mask, a way to shield the world from humans' vulnerabilities. But this can be more than just a mask—it can became a barrier. While trust can be offered coming from others, this can be met with hesitation, therefore, becoming a burden.

Uncertainty as a mask

But the silent betrayal wasn't one grand act that shattered my trust. It was the slow, almost invisible erosion of connection. Each moment I questioned myself, every time I let fear dictate my choices, I chipped away at the bond I had with others. The betrayal didn't come from malicious intent; it came from a place of internal chaos—a place where the insecurities ruled over the ability to be fully present and committed. But the insecurities in control. And In the most profound depths of the insecurities, I could see how they controlled me. The fear of inadequacy, the constant need for validation, and the way I held back from vulnerability—they all played a role in my betrayal. I doubted myself, and in that doubt, I doubted us. You couldn't offer stability or certainty because you hadn't yet found it within yourself.

Therefore, the consequences of uncertainty took root in our relationship; it was like a slow poison. It caused both people to question the bond they share and their worth. Your betrayal, born out of your insecurities, left me questioning myself. I wondered if I had done something wrong, if I had somehow caused you to lose trust in yourself. But in reality, your battle wasn't with me—it was with the deepest fears you harbored inside.

The truth is, I wanted to save you from your own uncertainty. I wanted to show you that my trust could help you rise above it. But in the end, no one can rescue another from their insecurities. That's a journey we all must take alone. And as your uncertainty consumed you, it ultimately consumed our relationship.

Thus, in the aftermath, I've come to understand that trust is not just about believing in someone else; it's also about their belief in themselves. You can't offer security or love if you're shackled by self-doubt. And while your uncertainty betrayed me, I realise now that it also betrayed you. It kept you from experiencing the depth of trust and connection we could have shared.

As I reflect on our broken trust, I am left with a profound lesson: trust can only be built on a foundation of self-awareness and emotional security. Without that, it is bound to crumble under the weight of uncertainty. I've learned that I can offer trust, but it's up to the other person to carry it, nurture it, and live up to the potential that trust creates.

I can only say that, in the end, your betrayal wasn't just about me—it was about the battle within yourself. And until that battle is won, trust will always be fragile, easily shattered by the tremors of insecurity.

Therefore, as I navigate through the labyrinth of my thoughts and experiences, I find that sharing my journey often requires a leap into the depths of vulnerability. Today, I wish to invite you into my past—specifically, into the shadows of my personal fears.

These fears have shaped me in ways I am only beginning to understand. They are not merely remnants of my past; they are reflections of my humanity. By sharing these fears with you, I hope to create a bridge of understanding, one that fosters connection and encourages introspection.

Join me as I unfold the stories that lie within these fears, revealing the lessons learned and the resilience gained along the way.

Fear of Vulnerability

Please allow me to share a personal experience dating someone years ago. I learned something precious about human behaviour and why people hide their true selves. People often hide their true selves to avoid being emotionally vulnerable by exposing their authentic thoughts and feelings, which may lead to criticism, rejection, or abandonment. The fear of abandonment, especially when there is a higher societal status, often exists as the fear of losing control of their environment, relationships, or even the people around them.

Fear of Judgment or Shame

During my dating days, as an observer, I noticed a common fear—the fear that one's honest thoughts, emotions, or desires might be seen as unworthy or shameful. This often led people to create a 'social mask,' presenting a more acceptable or appealing version of themselves.

I've often wondered why we, as human beings, feel the need to hide behind such masks. What drives us to conceal our true selves and replace authenticity with something we believe will be more acceptable? Let's explore this deeper.

Past Trauma or Rejection

When we experience rejection, abandonment, or emotional pain in the past, we may hide our true selves as a defense mechanism, trying to avoid those past experiences that trigger intense emotional pain, fear, and discomfort. However, trauma can be overwhelming, and it can cause physical and physiological responses leading to flashbacks, nightmares, or severe anxiety, where we as individuals feel as if we are reliving the event.

Self-deception and self-betrayal indeed represent some of the deepest forms of internal imprisonment. Losing one's integrity by denying personal truth or living in ways that violate one's values is a form of spiritual and psychological decay. This self-imposed destruction can be even more painful because it feels like a slow erosion from within, where the chains are not external but made from one's choices and denial.

Uncertainty as a mask

Fear of Losing Your Image

The fear of abandonment can extend to an intense fear of losing public image or reputation. For men and women in high-status positions, public perception often becomes closely tied to their sense of personal worth and growth. Any threat to their reputation can feel like a threat of abandonment, leading to defensive behaviors or an excessive concern about how others perceive them.

Never Forget How Far You've Come

Think of everything you've gotten through. You've pushed on, even in those moments when you felt you couldn't. Remember all the mornings you got out of bed, no matter how hard it was. Recall the times you wanted to give up, yet you made it through another day. Never forget the incredible strength you've gained and the resilience you've built along the way.

The joy of overcoming uncertainty is a profound emotional and mental experience that often comes after navigating challenging and unpredictable periods in your life.

This joy is not just about reaching a place of stability; it's about the transformation that happens within us as we face the unknown, adapt, and emerge stronger. Let's break down the different layers of this joy, reflecting on what it means to transcend uncertainty:

1. The Joy of Self-Discovery

Uncertainty pushes us out of our comfort zones, forcing us to confront our fears, limitations, and insecurities. As we overcome uncertainty, we discover parts of ourselves we never knew existed—strengths, talents, resilience, and courage. The joy comes from realising that we are capable of more than we thought possible.

Example:

"In the depths of uncertainty, I found parts of myself that had been hidden beneath layers of doubt. I discovered strength I never knew I had, and in that discovery, I found a profound joy. It was a joy born from knowing that no matter what life throws at me, I have the inner resources to navigate through it."

2. The Joy of Freedom from Fear

Uncertainty is often accompanied by fear—fear of the unknown, fear of failure, fear of making the wrong decisions. Overcoming uncertainty doesn't necessarily mean that the fear goes away, but it means that we learn to move forward despite it. The joy here is the liberation from the grip of fear, as we realise that we can embrace life's unpredictability with an open heart.

Uncertainty as a mask

Example:

"There was a time when uncertainty filled me with paralysing fear. But as I walked through the fog, I realised that fear was only as powerful as I allowed it to be. The joy of overcoming uncertainty is the freedom that comes from knowing that fear no longer controls you—it becomes just another challenge to face, not a wall to hide behind."

3. The Joy of Growth and Transformation

Facing uncertainty is one of the most powerful catalysts for personal growth. The joy that follows comes from the transformation that occurs within us—the way we think, the way we approach problems, the way we understand ourselves and the world. Overcoming uncertainty often leads to a renewed sense of purpose, clarity, and vision for the future.

Example:

"When I look back on the times of greatest uncertainty in my life, I realise hey were also the times of greatest growth. Each step forward, no matter how uncertain, transformed me in ways I never expected. The joy I feel now is not just for what I've accomplished but for who I've become along the way."

4. The Joy of Inner Peace and Confidence

Overcoming uncertainty often brings a sense of inner peace. There's a deep joy in knowing that, despite all the chaos and unpredictability, you found your way through. This experience builds a quiet confidence—a belief that, no matter what comes next, you will be able to handle it.

Example:

"In the midst of uncertainty, I often felt lost, as if I were navigating through a storm without a compass. But with each challenge I overcame, I found a sense of inner peace. The joy isn't just in reaching the shore—it's in knowing that I've become my own guide, confident in my ability to weather any storm."

5. The Joy of Appreciating the Present Moment

One of the hidden gifts of overcoming uncertainty is that it teaches us to value the present moment. The experience of not knowing what comes next can make us more mindful of the here and now. The joy comes from a newfound appreciation for the small, everyday moments that we may have once taken for granted.

Example:

"Living through uncertainty taught me to find joy in the present moment. Instead of worrying about what tomorrow might bring, I learned to celebrate the little things—the warmth of the sun on my face, the laughter of loved ones, the quiet moments of stillness. The joy of overcoming uncertainty is the gift of learning to truly live in the now."

6. The Joy of Reclaiming Power and Control

Uncertainty can make us feel powerless, as if we're at the mercy of forces beyond our control. But when we face it head-on, we reclaim our power. The joy here is in realising that we are not passive bystanders in our own lives. We have the strength to make choices, to adapt, and to shape our own destinies, no matter how unpredictable the circumstances.

Example:

"For so long, I felt like uncertainty was something that happened to me—a force I couldn't control. But as I learned to embrace it, I discovered the joy of taking back my power. It wasn't about controlling the outcome but about controlling my response. The joy was in knowing that I am the author of my own story."

7. The Joy of Inspiring Others

There is a unique joy that comes from knowing that your journey through uncertainty can inspire others. Your story becomes a beacon of hope, showing others that it is possible to find strength, resilience, and even joy in the most uncertain of times.

Example:

"I never imagined that my struggles with uncertainty would become a source of inspiration for others. But as I shared my journey, I saw the impact it had—how my story gave others the courage to face their own challenges. There's a deep joy in knowing that by overcoming my own uncertainties, I can help others find their way."

Bringing it all together, the joy of overcoming uncertainty isn't about reaching a final destination; it's about embracing the journey with all its twists and turns. It's about learning to dance in the rain, to find light in the darkness, and to discover that, within us, there is a wellspring of strength that can carry us through anything.

Uncertainty as a mask

WHILE THE WORLD IS
FILLED WITH UNCERTAINTY,

THERE NEED NOT BE UNCERTAINTY IN YOUR

HEART AND MIND

ABOUT WHAT IS **TRUE** AND WHAT IS NOT.

- Rusell M, Nelson

CHAPTER X

I Trusted You!

In this chapter of trust, I believed I could rely on myself—on my own decisions, instincts, and strength.

But the more I leaned on that trust, the more I began to doubt. It wasn't that others had failed me, but that I had betrayed my own belief in myself.

Every choice became clouded by uncertainty, every action weighed down by the fear that I couldn't follow through.

It wasn't just external doubt; it was the quiet insidious erosion of my own confidence, retreating deeper into the shadows of my insecurities.

I saw potential, strength, and someone who could be an anchor in my life. But what I didn't see—what I was hiding beneath the surface—were the layers of doubt and fear that would eventually unravel us both, my innerchild and my adult authenticity. Therefore, the mask I wore became a cage, both for me and those around me. I had built it to protect myself, to shield the world from my vulnerabilties, but in doing so, I trapped us both. They only saw the surface, the person I chose to show, the version of myself that seem certain, confident. But benneth that, the real me was unrevealing, slowly suffocatting under the weight of the wall I had duilt. And, yet, others wore their own mask.

The mask of someone trying to reach me, to connect, but unsure how to break through. In the end, it wasn't just the mask that kept us apart, it was the unravelling of both of us, torn between the selves we presented and the selves we hid.

As I navigate the complex terrain of my emotions, I've encountered a profound realisation that I feel compelled to share: the concept of emotional self-betrayal. Through my journey, I've uncovered several valuable insights highlighting how easily we can stray from our authentic selves, often without even realising it.

In this exploration, I want to shed light on the subtle ways we may undermine our emotional needs and values. I've come to recognise that understanding these patterns is not just an act of self-reflection but a necessary step toward reclaiming our true selves.

Throughout this chapter, I will share key points I've discovered about emotional self-betrayal.

Emotional Self-Betrayal

The Silent Sabotage of the Heart

Emotional self-betrayal occurs when we abandon our true feelings, needs, or desires in favor of external expectations, approval, or fear of confrontation.

It's a subtle yet profound way in which we compromise our own emotional well-being, often without fully realising it. This internal conflict can create deep wounds, manifesting as anxiety, resentment, or a lingering sense of dissatisfaction.

1. Recognising Emotional Self-Betrayal

At its core, emotional self-betrayal is the act of denying or suppressing our authentic emotional responses. This can happen in various ways:

- **Avoiding Conflict:** You may silence your needs to keep the peace in a relationship, telling yourself it's not worth the confrontation. Over time, this builds resentment and emotional distance.
- **People-pleasing:** Saying "yes" to others when you want to say "no" is a common form of emotional self-betrayal. You sacrifice your own boundaries and well-being to maintain approval or avoid disappointment from others.
- **Disconnection from Intuition:** This occurs when we ignore our gut feelings or instincts because they conflict with what others expect, leaving us disconnected from our true selves.

2. The Consequences of Betraying Yourself

The impact of emotional self-betrayal can be subtle at first, but over time, it can erode your sense of identity and self-worth. This disconnection from your inner truth may result in:

- **Internal Conflict:** A constant tug-of-war between your true feelings and the persona you present to the world can lead to emotional exhaustion, anxiety, or even depression.
- **Loss of Authenticity:** When you repeatedly ignore or betray your emotional needs, you lose touch with your true self. This disconnection can make it challenging to form authentic relationships or to experience joy and fulfillment.
- **Damaged Self-Trust:** Each time you dismiss your own emotions or compromise your values, you chip away at your ability to trust yourself. You may begin to question your own instincts and judgment, which can create a cycle of dependency on others for validation.

3. Healing from Emotional Self-Betrayal

Healing requires acknowledging how you've compromised your emotions and actively choosing to reconnect with your inner self.

Critical steps to recovery include:

- **Reclaiming Your Voice:** Start by expressing your true feelings in small, manageable ways. Whether saying "no" when you need to or speaking up about something that matters, each act of honesty strengthens your emotional integrity.
- **Setting Boundaries:** Establishing and maintaining boundaries is crucial for preventing future self-betrayal. Boundaries protect your emotional space and allow you to honor your needs without guilt or fear of rejection.
- **Practicing Self-Compassion:** Forgive yourself for the times you've compromised your emotions in the past. Recognise that emotional self-betrayal is often rooted in fear or a desire to protect yourself from pain, and offer yourself kindness as you navigate this healing process.
- **Trusting Your Intuition:** Reconnect with your inner voice by paying attention to your instincts. Learning to trust your feelings and judgments is a powerful step toward reclaiming your emotional autonomy.

4. Self-Reclamation After Betrayal

The journey of healing from emotional self-betrayal ultimately leads to a process of self-reclamation. You reclaim your personal power by acknowledging your past compromises and choosing to honor your emotions moving forward. This new commitment to emotional authenticity enables you to live a life aligned with your true self, fostering deeper connections and a sense of inner peace.

When you stop betraying yourself, you cultivate a life in which your emotional truth takes precedence. This space of emotional honesty opens the door to greater self-awareness, healthier relationships, and lasting inner growth.

Understanding Self-Emotional Betrayal

Self-emotional betrayal is a powerful and often painful concept that many people experience, sometimes without even realising it. It occurs when we consciously or unconsciously go against our own feelings, needs, values, or boundaries, often in an attempt to please others, avoid conflict, or fit into certain expectations. This internal betrayal can manifest in various ways, leading to a disconnect between our true selves and the life we're living.

1. Ignoring Your Own Needs

One of the most common forms of self-emotional betrayal is neglecting your own needs to prioritise others' desires or expectations. This can happen in relationships, at work, or even in everyday interactions. Over time, consistently putting others first can lead to feelings of resentment, burnout, and a loss of self-identity.

Example:

"Every time I said 'yes' when I wanted to say 'no,' I betrayed myself a little more. I became a stranger to my own needs, sacrificing my well-being to meet the expectations of others."

Key Concept: Carl Jung explored the idea of the shadow self, which includes parts of ourselves that we deny or repress. This can be seen as a form of self-betrayal, where we deny our true feelings, desires, or instincts to maintain a socially acceptable persona.

2. Suppressing Your True Feelings

Another form of self-betrayal occurs when we suppress our true emotions to appear strong, agreeable, or acceptable. This could mean hiding your sadness behind a smile, not voicing your true opinions, or pretending to be happy in situations where you're hurting inside. The cost of this suppression is high, often leading to internal conflict, anxiety, or even depression.

Example:

"I convinced myself that if I just kept smiling, the pain would go away. But the more I pushed my feelings down, the more they festered, until I couldn't recognise the person I had become. My silence was my greatest betrayal."

Key Concept: In her book *The Dance of Anger*, Harriet Lerner explores how we often betray our true feelings to avoid conflict, leading to emotional disconnection and resentment.

3. Settling for Less Than You Deserve

Self-emotional betrayal also happens when you settle for less than you deserve, whether in relationships, career, or life choices. This might include staying in a toxic relationship, accepting a job that doesn't fulfill you, or remaining in situations that make you unhappy, all because you believe you don't deserve better.

Example:

"I stayed in a relationship that drained me because I thought it was the best I could do. Deep down, I knew I was betraying my desire for genuine love and respect, but I was too afraid to demand more."

Key Concept: In *The Way of Integrity*, Martha Beck discusses how ignoring our inner truth leads to a sense of being lost, which can be seen as a form of self-betrayal. She encourages readers to find their way back to their authentic selves by listening to their inner guidance.

4. Denying Your Authentic Self

Often, we betray ourselves by not living authentically—by hiding parts of who we are to fit into societal norms, family expectations, or peer pressure. This can involve everything from pretending to enjoy activities you don't like, to choosing a career that doesn't align with your passions, to hiding aspects of your identity to avoid judgment.

Example:

"For years, I wore a mask to fit into the world around me. I was afraid that showing my true self would lead to rejection. But every day that I hid, I felt a little more lost. The biggest betrayal was pretending to be someone I wasn't."

Key Concept: Brené Brown's work, particularly in books like *The Gifts of Imperfection* and *Daring Greatly*, explores how we betray ourselves by conforming to societal expectations and suppressing our true selves to fit in. She discusses the importance of vulnerability, authenticity, and self-compassion.

5. Ignoring Your Inner Voice

Self-betrayal can also occur when we ignore our intuition—the inner voice that tells us when something isn't right. This might mean staying silent when you should speak up, or continuing down a path that doesn't feel aligned with your true purpose, simply because it's easier than facing the truth.

Example:

"I knew deep down that the path I was on wasn't right for me, but I ignored that inner voice. I convinced myself that it was just fear talking, but in reality, I was betraying the truth of who I was meant to be."

Key Concept: In *The Four Agreements*, Don Miguel Ruiz addresses how we betray ourselves by accepting self-limiting beliefs and trying to please others. His concept of domestication is similar to self-betrayal, where we abandon our authenticity to meet external expectations.

Consequences of Self-Emotional Betrayal

1. Emotional Exhaustion

Constantly going against your own feelings can lead to emotional exhaustion. The energy it takes to maintain a facade, suppress your needs, or ignore your intuition can leave you feeling drained, both mentally and physically.

2. Loss of Self-Identity

Over time, self-betrayal can erode your sense of self. You may start to lose touch with who you really are, what you truly want, and what brings you joy. This loss of identity can lead to a feeling of emptiness or disconnection from your own life.

3. Lowered Self-Esteem

When you consistently betray your own emotions, you send yourself the message that your feelings, needs, and desires are not important. This can significantly lower your self-esteem and self-worth, making it even harder to break the cycle of self-betrayal.

4. Mental Health Struggles

The internal conflict caused by self-betrayal can contribute to anxiety, depression, and other mental health challenges. The disconnect between your true self and the life you're living can create a deep sense of inner turmoil.

Healing from Self-Emotional Betrayal

1. Reconnect with Your Inner Self

Begin by reconnecting with your true emotions, desires, and values. Spend time alone, journal your thoughts, meditate, or simply sit in silence to get back in touch with what's really going on inside you.

Prompt:

"What are the things you truly want, but have been ignoring or denying for the sake of others? What would happen if you gave yourself permission to honor those desires?"

2. Set Boundaries

Learn to set boundaries that protect your emotional well-being. This might mean saying 'no' more often, prioritising self-care, or distancing yourself from relationships that demand too much of you without giving anything in return.

3. Practice Self-Compassion

Healing from self-betrayal requires self-compassion. Recognise that you made the choices you did because you were trying to survive, to fit in, or to avoid pain. Forgive yourself for the times you put others above yourself and commit to making healthier choices moving forward.

4. Honour Your Authenticity

Start small by making choices that align with your true self. Speak your truth, pursue your passions, and live in a way that feels authentic to you. Each step you take towards honouring your own emotions will strengthen your self-connection.

Affirmation:

"I am worthy of living a life that aligns with my true feelings, needs, and desires. I choose to honour my emotions and live authentically."

5. Seek Support

Sometimes, the patterns of self-betrayal run deep, especially if they've been ingrained over years or decades. Therapy, coaching, or support groups can provide guidance and accountability as you learn to reconnect with yourself.

CHAPER XI

Practical Tools for Self-Connection After Consequential Self-Dishonour

1. Mindful Reflection and Journaling

Purpose: Journaling can help untangle the emotions tied to self-dishonour and provide clarity about what needs to be healed. By reflecting on your actions, thoughts, and feelings, you can reconnect with your authentic self.

How to Practice: Set aside quiet time each day for reflection. Ask yourself deep questions like:

"When did I feel disconnected from myself the most?"

"What feelings or needs have I been ignoring?"

"What does my heart need from me right now?"

Journaling Prompt:

"Reflect on a moment when you ignored your own needs for the sake of others. How did it feel in that moment? How do you feel now looking back? What could you have done differently to honor yourself?"

2. Breathing and Grounding Exercises

Purpose: Self-dishonour can manifest physically, creating tension and disconnection in the body. Breathwork and grounding exercises help you re-establish emotional and physical connection with yourself.

Breathing Exercise: Sit comfortably, take a deep breath in for a count of four, hold for four, and exhale for a count of four. Focus on releasing tension with each exhale.

Grounding Exercise: Stand or sit with your feet flat on the floor. Visualize roots growing from your feet deep into the earth, providing you with stability and connection to your true self. With every breath, feel yourself becoming more grounded.

Goal: To reconnect your physical body with your emotional self and create a space where you feel safe and present in the moment.

3. Setting Boundaries with Compassion

Purpose: Establishing healthy boundaries is key to reclaiming your emotional space and protecting your well-being after experiencing self-dishonour. Boundaries reflect self-respect and remind you that your needs matter.

How to Practice: Identify situations where you feel compromised or where your emotional needs are not being honoured. Practice saying "no" or expressing your needs calmly, without guilt.

Example:

"I need some time alone to recharge."

"I value our relationship, but I cannot continue this conversation right now."

Goal: To honour your emotional limits and practice self-compassion without feeling the need to apologise for your needs.

4. Self-Compassion and Forgiveness Rituals

Purpose: Self-compassion is essential for reconnecting after self-dishonour. Embrace the practice of forgiving yourself for past mistakes and embracing your humanity.

How to Practice: Stand in front of a mirror, look into your own eyes, and speak kindly to yourself. You might say:

"I forgive myself for any harm I've caused myself."

"I recognise that I was doing the best I could with what I knew."

"I am worthy of compassion and understanding."

Goal: To acknowledge your humanity and show yourself the love and grace you deserve, creating a healing environment for self-reconnection.

5. Reconnecting with Your Intuition

Purpose: Rebuilding trust with yourself requires reconnecting with your inner voice, your intuition. Trusting your gut feelings and learning to honour them will guide you back to your authentic self.

How to Practice: Start by asking yourself questions like, "What do I truly need right now?" or "What does my heart want?" Listen closely to your body's responses and practice making small decisions based on what feels right, not out of obligation or fear.

Goal: To rebuild your inner trust and connection to your emotions, validating your desires and needs.

Empowering Affirmations and Mantras

1. Affirmations for Self-Worth

- *"I am worthy of love, respect, and compassion."*

- *"I honor my feelings and trust my intuition."*

- "I deserve to take up space and have my needs met."

2. Affirmations for Self-Connection

- "I am re-establishing my bond with myself, one step at a time."

- "I trust myself, even when I am uncertain."

- "Every day, I grow closer to the person I am meant to be."

3. Mantras for Healing

- "I forgive myself for all the times I've betrayed my own heart."

- "I am healing, and I allow myself to feel fully."

- "I am not defined by my past mistakes; I am defined by the strength of my growth."

4. Affirmations for Emotional Freedom

- "I release guilt and shame; they do not belong to me."

- "I have the power to change my relationship with myself."

- "I am free to live authentically and honour my emotions."

Combining These Practices

As you incorporate these practical tools and affirmations into your life, the journey of reconnection will start to feel more natural. Remember, healing from self-dishonour isn't an overnight process—it's about showing up for yourself every day, even when it feels difficult.

Self-Reflection Exercise:

Here's a journal prompt for you. Take some time to create a quiet space for yourself, free from distractions. Grab your journal and reflect on the following:

"Think about a time when you felt you betrayed your own beliefs or doubted your self-worth. What led to that moment, and how did it impact you? Write about what you've learned from the experience and what steps you can take to honour yourself moving forward. Then, write down three affirmations that reinforce your self-worth, and commit to repeating them daily as a reminder of your strength and value."

Allow yourself to write freely and without judgment—this is your space for reflection and growth.

CHAPTER XII

Time and potential—vital life forces wanting to break free

Breaking through to freedom is the moment you cast off the constraints of fear, doubt, and external expectations, stepping into a space of boundless possibility. It's a powerful transformation where the mind no longer clings to past limitations, and the heart embraces the unknown with courage and hope.

Breaking through to freedom is a deeply transformative experience, often marked by a sense of release, clarity, and empowerment. It feels like shedding the weight of limitations—whether those are internal fears, societal expectations, or emotional baggage.

This process involves moving through discomfort and uncertainty, but on the other side is a feeling of liberation that brings peace and personal autonomy.

This freedom allows you to redefine who you are and opens the door to living authentically, unburdened by old patterns. In essence, breaking through to freedom is reclaiming your power and unlocking your full potential.

Emotionally, it's a mix of relief and exhilaration. Relief comes from finally letting go of what has been holding you back, while exhilaration stems from the new possibilities that emerge once you've crossed that threshold.

Time and potential—vital life forces wanting to break free

You may feel lighter as if a burden has been lifted, and more open to exploring new facets of life, untethered by past restraints.

When considering time versus the potential of freedom, there's an inherent tension between the two.

Time often feels like a constraint—moving forward without pause, pushing us to confront the realities of our circumstances, and imposing limits on how long we can stay in a place of comfort or avoidance.

On the other hand, freedom represents boundless possibility, a state of being that transcends those limitations and offers the chance to live authentically and fully.

Time as an Opponent to Freedom

Time can appear to work against our sense of freedom because it brings deadlines, aging, and the weight of life's responsibilities. As we grow older, societal expectations often intensify—pushing us to make decisions quickly, adhere to norms, or settle into roles that may feel limiting.

The ticking of the clock can become a reminder of all that remains undone, feeding fears of missing out on life's potential. In this sense, time can feel like a barrier to fully embracing the expansiveness of freedom, locking us into routines or obligations that suppress our desire to break free.

Time as an Ally to Freedom

However, time also holds the potential to be an ally in the pursuit of freedom. With each passing moment, we are granted the opportunity to evolve, to reflect on our past, and to make conscious choices that move us closer to liberation.

Time allows for growth and the cultivation of wisdom. As we navigate through life's stages, we learn to release others' expectations and embrace the journey toward personal freedom at our own pace.

What initially felt like a race against time can transform into an unfolding process of self-discovery and reclamation.

Balancing the Two

The key to navigating this tension lies in recognising that freedom cannot be achieved in spite of time but through it. Freedom is a continual process of making intentional choices that align with your values and desires, even within the framework of time. It's not about outrunning the clock but about using your moments to create a life that feels free and fulfilling.

Time and potential—vital life forces wanting to break free

Ultimately, the potential of freedom grows as you learn to live in harmony with time—not fighting against its flow but using it as a tool for growth, reflection, and transformation.

There's also a profound sense of empowerment: knowing that you've overcome something significant allows you to trust yourself more deeply. This creates space for authentic self-expression and living more in line with your true desires rather than being confined by past fears or doubts.

The journey to freedom often starts with internal reflection and ends with a redefinition of what freedom means for you beyond external expectations. It can be a journey of self-discovery, resilience, and ultimately, reclamation of your own narrative.

The Nature of Time as an Opponent

This is such a profound and insightful concept! Exploring how time functions as an opponent—especially in the context of emotional and intellectual progress—reveals the delicate dance between our inner world and external environments. Let's break this down and see how imbalance in managing time and external influences can impact us.

When we view time as an opponent, it often feels like we're in a constant race against it. This perspective can arise when we:

- Feel overwhelmed by deadlines, obligations, and societal pressures.
- Experience regret or anxiety about the past and the future.
- Become overly focused on "running out of time" to achieve personal or professional goals.

This pressure can create a sense of urgency that disrupts our emotional balance, causing stress and even burnout. The more we struggle against time, the less we are able to experience the present moment fully, which can be detrimental to our overall well-being

The Impact on Emotional Progress

1. Emotional Exhaustion and Disconnection

- When time feels like an opponent, we may neglect our emotional needs, focusing instead on what needs to be done rather than how we feel. This can lead to emotional exhaustion, leaving us feeling disconnected from ourselves.
- **Example**: Constantly rushing to meet deadlines might cause you to suppress your emotions, leading

Time and potential—vital life forces wanting to break free

to pent-up stress and anxiety. Over time, this can erode your sense of self-connection and diminish emotional resilience.

2. Anxiety and Self-Doubt

- A relentless focus on time can fuel anxiety, especially when we feel like we're falling behind in life. The comparison to others' timelines or societal expectations can trigger self-doubt and diminish self-worth.
- **Example**: Feeling pressured to achieve certain milestones by a specific age can lead to feelings of inadequacy, overshadowing personal progress and self-acceptance.

The Impact on Intellectual Progress

1. Stifling Creativity and Curiosity

- When time becomes a stressor, it can stifle creativity. The mind shifts from exploring possibilities to focusing on efficiency and productivity, which can limit intellectual growth.
- **Example**: If you're always focused on "getting things done," you may not give yourself the space to think freely, reflect deeply, or explore new ideas that don't have immediate outcomes.

2. Surface-Level Learning and Rushed Decisions

- Intellectual growth requires patience, reflection, and curiosity. Viewing time as an opponent can lead to surface-level learning, where the focus is on quickly acquiring knowledge rather than deeply understanding it.
- **Example**: In an effort to quickly gain new skills or knowledge, you may rush through courses or books, missing the deeper insights that come from a more thoughtful, deliberate approach.

The Role of External Environments

Balancing time with the influence of external environments is crucial. Our surroundings, including the people we interact with and the spaces we inhabit, significantly shape our emotional and intellectual state. When there's an imbalance, it can either amplify the stress associated with time or help alleviate it.

1. Positive External Influences for Balance

- Supportive Relationships: Surrounding yourself with people who encourage taking breaks, reflecting, and celebrating small achievements can counteract the stress of time pressure.

- Nurturing Environments: Creating physical spaces that promote calmness, such as a cozy reading nook or a serene outdoor setting, can help you slow down and reconnect with yourself.

2. Negative External Influences that Amplify Pressure

- Toxic Environments: Being around individuals who constantly emphasise productivity and achievement can exacerbate the feeling of time as an opponent, leading to heightened anxiety.
- Digital Overload: Excessive use of social media, where everyone seems to be achieving something, can create a false sense of urgency, making you feel like you're always behind.

How to Achieve Balance: Practical Strategies

1. Mindful Time Management

- Shift your perception of time from an opponent to a companion. Use time as a tool to prioritise what matters most to you, rather than letting it dictate your actions.
- Practice: Use techniques like the Pomodoro Technique or time blocking, not to race against

time, but to create dedicated periods for work, rest, and self-reflection.

2. Create Buffer Zones for Emotional Reflection

- Carve out intentional moments in your day for emotional check-ins. This could be through journaling, meditation, or simply pausing to ask yourself how you're feeling.
- Practice: Set aside 10-15 minutes at the beginning or end of each day to reflect on your emotions, celebrating small wins, and acknowledging any challenges.

3. Cultivate an Intellectual Growth Mindset

- Embrace the process of learning without focusing solely on the outcome. Allow yourself to explore subjects and hobbies for the sake of curiosity, not productivity.
- Practice: Dedicate time each week to explore something new without any pressure to excel—whether it's reading a book, learning a new language, or simply watching a documentary.

4. Leverage Your Environment for Balance

- Curate your surroundings to be a source of support rather than pressure. Limit exposure to environments that trigger time-related anxiety, and gravitate toward spaces that foster peace and creativity.
- Practice: Declutter your space, add elements that inspire calm (like plants, art, or soft lighting), and set boundaries with people who pressure you into urgency.

By shifting your perception of time from an adversary to an ally and balancing it with positive external influences, you can transform how you approach emotional and intellectual growth. It's about finding harmony—moving at a pace that aligns with your inner needs instead of rushing to match the world's clock.

Remember, time can be either a relentless critic or a gentle guide—the choice lies in how you engage with it.

The Trap of Misplaced Focus

Have you ever ended the day feeling completely drained, only to realise that most of your energy was spent on worries, regrets, or things that ultimately didn't matter?

This is the trap of misplaced focus—a silent thief that steals our time, drains our emotional reserves, and leaves us feeling unfulfilled. When we get caught in this trap, we unintentionally pour our energy into thoughts and activities that do not align with our true desires and purpose. It's like watering weeds in the garden of our mind, allowing them to overgrow and overshadow the flowers of joy, growth, and self-connection.

1. Understanding Misplaced Focus

We live in a world where distractions are endless, from the constant ping of notifications to the pressures of social media and societal expectations. These external forces can easily pull us into a cycle of misplaced focus, where we prioritise what seems urgent over what is truly important.

Example: Imagine spending hours scrolling through social media, comparing your life to others, and worrying about not being "enough." This not only drains your energy but also pulls your attention away from what truly fulfills you—be it your personal growth, relationships, or passions.

2. The Emotional Toll of Distractions

When our focus is scattered on things that don't serve us, it affects our emotional well-being. Misplaced focus often leads to:

- **Increased Anxiety:** Constantly worrying about the future or dwelling on the past.
- **Self-Doubt:** Feeling inadequate because we are comparing ourselves to unrealistic standards.
- **Emotional Exhaustion:** Wasting energy on things beyond our control, leaving us drained and disconnected.

Reflection: Ask yourself—How often do you let negative thoughts or external pressures control your focus? Are you investing your emotional energy in things that truly matter to you?

3. Signs You're Caught in the Trap

To break free from this cycle, it's important to recognize the signs of misplaced focus:

- **Endless Rumination:** Overthinking past mistakes or future uncertainties.
- **Procrastination:** Filling your time with low-value tasks to avoid confronting important but challenging goals.
- **Seeking External Validation:** Focusing on pleasing others rather than honouring your own needs and desires.
- **Practical Insight:** Remember, what you focus on grows. If you focus on your fears and limitations, they will expand. If you focus on your strengths

and opportunities, you will open the doors to growth.

4. Reclaiming Your Focus: Shifting from Reaction to Intention

To break free from the trap of misplaced focus, we need to shift from a reactive mindset to one of intention. This means consciously deciding where to direct our attention and energy.

Strategies for Reclaiming Your Focus:

- **Mindful Awareness:** Start each day with a moment of reflection. Ask yourself: "What do I want to focus on today that will bring me closer to my goals and fulfillment?"
- **The Art of Letting Go:** Learn to release thoughts that drain you. Visualize them as clouds passing by, and gently redirect your focus to something that uplifts you.
- **Focus on What You Can Control:** Instead of wasting energy on things beyond your control, channel that energy into what you can change, like your attitude, effort, and actions.

5. Transforming Misplaced Focus into Empowered Action

The key to breaking free from the trap is to transform misplaced focus into empowered action. This means shifting from being a passive observer of your thoughts to an active participant in your life.

Action Steps:

- **Set Clear Priorities:** Define what truly matters to you, whether it's personal growth, relationships, or creative projects. Align your daily actions with these priorities.
- **Create Boundaries:** Protect your mental space by setting boundaries with people, activities, or thoughts that drain your energy.
- **Practice Gratitude:** Focus on what you have, not what you lack. Gratitude redirects your attention to abundance, which can empower and uplift your spirit.

Empowering Affirmation:

"I choose to focus my energy on what aligns with my highest purpose. I release distractions and embrace clarity."

6. Closing Reflection: Embracing a Focused Life

Imagine the possibilities when you reclaim your focus and direct it toward what truly matters. By breaking free from the trap of misplaced focus, you open up space for growth, peace, and fulfillment. Each moment becomes an opportunity to realign with your true self and live with intention.

Reflective Question:

"What would your life look like if you fully committed to focusing on what truly matters to you?"

CHAPTER XIII

My Terms, My Conditions, My Loss

Dear Reader,

There comes a time in everyone's journey when we must confront the reality of life's terms.

For many, this means accepting external conditions, societal pressures, or the weight of others' expectations. But what happens when we choose to reject those imposed standards and set our own?

What happens when we take ownership not only of our victories but also of our losses?

Living on my terms hasn't always been easy. It required courage to step away from the mold that was expected of me and create a life shaped by my own values.

To live by my conditions means embracing my imperfections, honouring my boundaries, and following the unique rhythm of my path. It means standing tall even when the world pushes back and learning to listen to my inner voice when doubt whispers louder.

This journey, however, has not been without loss. I've had to leave behind people, places, and dreams that no longer aligned with who I've become.

Loss is inevitable when we grow into our authentic selves. Yet, I've learned that loss isn't the end; it's a release. It's the shedding of the old to make space for the new, even if that newness comes wrapped in uncertainty or pain.

Loss has taught me resilience. It has shown me the beauty of impermanence and the strength required to let go of what no longer serves me. Living on my term means accepting that not everyone will understand the choices I've made and that not every relationship will endure.

But in this space of self-ownership, I've discovered a freedom that makes the pain of loss worthwhile.

I want to share this journey with you, not as a guide but as a witness to the power of living authentically.

If you've ever felt the pull to live on your own terms—despite the losses you may face along the way—I hope you find solace in knowing that you are not alone. The road may be challenging, but the rewards are immeasurable.

The Power of Embracing Your Own Terms After Feeling Defeated

This is a profound and empowering topic! Let's explore the power of embracing your own terms and conditions after feeling defeated.

This concept is all about reclaiming your sense of self and redefining your journey, especially after facing setbacks that made you feel like you lost your way or missed out on victory. It's about recognizing that true victory is not in the approval of others, or external achievements, it is in living life authentically on your own terms.

Redefining Victory on Your Own Terms

There are moments in life when it feels like everything has slipped away—the victories, the recognition, the dreams you once held close. Maybe it was a relationship that ended, a career setback, or a personal goal that slipped through your fingers.

These experiences can leave you questioning your worth, your path, and your ability to rise again. But what if true strength lies not in the victories you thought you lost, but in the courage to start anew on your own terms?

When you embrace your own terms and conditions after what feels like a loss, you reclaim your narrative. You decide not to be defined by past defeats or the expectations of others. Instead, you become the author of your life story, creating rules that reflect your values, passions, and inner truth.

My Terms, My Conditions, My Loss

1. Understanding the Illusion of Defeat

The first step to reclaiming your power is understanding that defeat is often a matter of perspective. What you perceive as a loss may actually be a redirection, a call to align with something greater.

- **Reframing Failure:** Instead of seeing setbacks as the end, view them as lessons that guide you closer to your authentic path.

- **Question to Reflect On:** What if what you thought was a loss was actually a hidden blessing, guiding you toward your true purpose?

2. The Liberation of Letting Go

Before you can embrace your own terms, it's essential to let go of the old ones that no longer serve you. This includes societal pressures, outdated beliefs, and the expectations of others.

- **Exercise:** Take a piece of paper and write down the rules or expectations you've been trying to live up to. Next to each one, write whether it aligns with your authentic self. If it doesn't, cross it out.
- **Empowering Thought:** I release the need to live by anyone else's rules. I am free to create my own path.

3. Crafting Your New Terms and Conditions

The beauty of embracing your own terms is that you get to define what success, happiness, and fulfillment mean to you. This is your chance to rewrite the script of your life.

Steps to Define Your Own Terms:

1. **Identify Your Core Values:** What truly matters to you? Family, creativity, peace, freedom? Let these guide your decisions.
2. **Set Non-Negotiables:** Determine the boundaries you need to honour your well-being, such as saying no to draining commitments or prioritising self-care.
3. **Declare Your Intentions:** Write a personal manifesto or set of "terms and conditions" that reflect how you want to live your life moving forward.

Example Statement: I am no longer defined by my past losses. I choose to live boldly, guided by my own values and dreams.

4. Turning Setbacks into Stepping Stones

When you embrace your own terms, even the most painful setbacks can become stepping stones. They teach you resilience, self-reliance, and the power to rebuild.

Transformative Mindset:

- **From Victim to Victor:** Shift from asking, "Why did this happen to me?" to "What is this teaching me?"
- **Celebrate Small Wins:** Recognise that every step forward, no matter how small, is a victory when it's on your own terms.
- **Empowering Thought:** Every setback is an invitation to rise stronger, not by the standards of others, but by the light of my own soul.

5. The Joy of Living Authentically

When you start living life on your own terms, you unlock a deep sense of freedom and joy. This joy doesn't come from external achievements but from the peace of knowing you are living in alignment with your true self.

- **Daily Practice:** Each morning, set an intention to honour your own terms. It could be as simple as choosing joy over obligation or peace over perfection.
- **Reflective Question:** What would your life look like if you fully embraced your own terms and conditions? How would it feel to release the need for external validation?

6. Embracing Self-Forgiveness and Compassion

Living by your own terms also means forgiving yourself for the times you didn't. It's about showing compassion for your past decisions and understanding that every choice led you to this moment of awakening.

- **Self-Forgiveness Exercise:** Write a letter to yourself, forgiving past mistakes and celebrating your decision to now live on your own terms.
- **Empowering Thought:** I am no longer bound by my past. I embrace the power to choose differently and live authentically.

In conclusion, the power of embracing your own terms and conditions lies in the liberation it brings. It's a journey of reclaiming your voice, your choices, and your life.

The moment you decide to define your path, not by past failures, but by the feedback and the potential of your own dreams, you step into a life of true freedom.

A final reflection for us — my dear friend, reader, and myself:

"What's one rule or belief we can let go of today, so we can live life on our own terms?"

If you are feeling lost, abandoned or forgotten –

fear NOT. The Good Shepherd will find you.

HE WILL LIFT YOU

upon his shoulders, and He will carry you home.

- Dieter F. Uchtdorf

A Letter to My Readers and My Old Self

As I write these final words, I find myself pausing for a moment of quiet reflection. This book has been more than just a story—it's been a journey of self-discovery, transformation, and healing. And now, as we reach the end, I want to take a moment to bid farewell—to you, my dear reader, and to the version of myself that I am finally letting go of.

To the Old Me, I Say Thank You

You were the one who walked through life with fear, doubt, and pain. You carried the weight of past mistakes, and yet, you showed up every day. Despite the confusion and the hurt, you did the best you could. You fought battles I never imagined, and your strength is a part of me that I will never forget. Without you, there would be no path to freedom, no lessons learned, and no growth to celebrate.

But now, I must say goodbye.

It's not because you were wrong, but because I've outgrown the person you were. I have learned to forgive, to trust, and to believe in my own worth. The woman I am today no longer needs to carry the burdens that once defined you. I choose to honour you by letting you go with love, for you have paved the way for this new chapter.

To you, my reader, I offer my deepest gratitude.

Thank you for taking this journey with me, for allowing me to share the raw, vulnerable pieces of my heart. In these pages, I hope you've found reflections of your own struggles, triumphs, and growth. I hope you've felt the warmth of understanding and the comfort of knowing that you, too, have the power to let go of the old and embrace the new.

As I bid farewell to the version of myself that held onto the past, I invite you to do the same. I hope this book has encouraged you to release what no longer serves you, to forgive yourself for the choices you once regretted, and to step boldly into the future that awaits.

My Terms, My Conditions, My Loss

This farewell is not a loss. It is a gift. It is the space where new beginnings can take root, where healing can flourish, and where the truest version of ourselves can emerge.

So, as we close this chapter, I leave you with one final thought: every ending holds the promise of a new beginning. The woman I am now is only the beginning of the woman I am becoming. And so, with courage and love, I step forward into my next chapter. May you do the same.

With all my heart,

Bethsaida Hingston

Conclusion

Embracing the Journey Ahead

As we reach the end of this book, I'm reminded that the journey we've shared together is not an ending—it's a new beginning. The pages we've turned, the stories we've explored, and the lessons we've uncovered are just the first steps of an ongoing journey that holds limitless possibilities.

This book has been my story—one of healing, of reclaiming my freedom, and of embracing the woman I am today. Along this path, I've experienced profound transformations, both personally and professionally. From overcoming the emotional scars of my past to finding the strength to rebuild my future, I've achieved what I once thought was impossible.

My small business has flourished into a meaningful venture that supports so many. I've had the privilege of traveling the world, sharing my journey at global mental health summits, and becoming a Life Coach—helping incredible souls discover new, positive paths in their lives. Most importantly, I've found a deep sense of peace and connection within myself—something that once felt unattainable.

These successes are not the end of my story; they are just the beginning. This journey continues, as does yours. Healing is not a destination—it is a process, a continual unfolding of the person you are becoming. The work we've done together in these pages, the lessons we've shared, are only stepping stones to the future that awaits us.

As I've said goodbye to the old version of myself, you too have the power to let go of what no longer serves you. You have the power to rewrite your story, to transform your struggles into strengths, and to embrace the full potential of your life. You don't need to be perfect, but you do need to be willing to keep moving forward with courage, even when the path ahead feels uncertain.

Remember, the greatest successes are not measured by external achievements, but by the inner peace, growth, and freedom we create within ourselves. You are worthy of all that you desire. You are capable of the most profound transformation. Your best chapters are yet to be written.

So, with love, gratitude, and deep encouragement, I thank you for walking this journey with me. No matter where

Conclusion

life takes you, know that you are not alone. You have everything within you to create the life you dream of.

My heartfelt thanks to everyone around the world who journeyed with me through The Way to Freedom.

With all my heart,

Bethsaida Hingston

About The Author

Bethsaida Hingston (born Bethsaida Flores Cabrera in 1971) grew up under the loving guidance of her parents, Filemon Flores Velasco and Lourdes Cabrera de Flores. Their wisdom and unwavering support instilled in her the values of resilience, kindness, and the pursuit of freedom. After marrying an Australian man, she became Bethsaida Hingston, continuing to build her life around the principles her parents had taught her.

The loss of her father during the COVID-19 pandemic brought profound uncertainty, yet the teachings of both her parents served as her compass, guiding her toward a renewed sense of freedom and inner strength.

Bethsaida's journey has been one of transformation, embracing vulnerability as a source of strength and finding purpose in helping others. She is a Life Coach, Founder of Betsy's Special Needs Services, and the author of *The Way to Freedom*. Her work reflects the legacy of her parents' lessons—turning challenges into growth and inspiring others to discover their own paths to emotional freedom and resilience.

Acknowledgements

This book would not have been possible without the support and encouragement of incredible people. First and foremost, I want to thank my parents, whose endless love, wisdom, and belief in me have always been my guiding light. To my amazing editor, Maddie, your insightful feedback and patience helped transform this manuscript into something far better than I could have imagined. I also want to thank my writing group—Natasa Denman, and Stuart Denman—for their sharp critiques and constant motivation. Your encouragement kept me going during the toughest moments. A heartfelt thank you to my many loving friends, for your unwavering support and for always reminding me to believe in myself, even when I doubted. Finally, to my readers—thank you for sharing this journey with me. Your feedback and enthusiasm mean the world.

References

Bograd, M.(1998). Enmeshment, fusion, or relatedness? Journal of Psychotherapy & The Family

Colapinto, J. (2015). Structural family therapy. I T. Sexton & J. Lebow (Eds.), Handbook of family therapy (pp. 120-130). New York: Routledge.

Reference to Emotional Boundaries: [Remi Pearson, Founder of the Coaching Institute,- Meta Dynamics – Critical Alignment Model]

[Carl Jung- "The Archetypes and the Collective Unconscious"] Jung's work emphasizes the importance of connecting with the unconscious mind, where deeper aspects of the self are stored. He introduces the idea of individualisation, a process where one integrates the conscious and unconscious parts of the self for personal growth and wholeness.]

[Rumi- " The Essential Rumi" The Sufi mystic Rumi often wrote about the connection between the self and the divine within, expressing a deep sense of inner awareness and love that transcends the external world.]

[Thich Nhat Hanh- "The Miracle of Mindfulness" A Vietnamese Buddhist monk, Hanh speaks extensively about cultivating mindfulness and conscious awareness to connect deeply with oneself, leading to inner peace and compassion for others.]

Salvador Munichin (1974) used the term enmeshment to describe the overinvolved relationships that develop from diffuse boundaries within family systems and between family members and other systems.

Dr Heidi Keller (Germany) Institute of Psychology, Osnabruck University, 49069 Osnabruck, Germany (relatedness), expert in child psychology and cultural studies, in particular the use the culturally loaded attachment theory.

Bograd, M.(1998). Enmeshment, fusion, or relatedness? Journal of Psychotherapy & The Family Colapinto, J. (2015). Structural family therapy. I T. Sexton & J. Lebow (Eds.), Handbook of family therapy (pp. 120-130). New York: Routledge.

Bograd, M.(1998). Enmeshment, fusion, or relatedness? Journal of Psychotherapy & The Family

References

Colapinto, J. (2015). Structural family therapy. I T. Sexton & J. Lebow (Eds.), Handbook of family therapy (pp. 120-130). New York: Routledg

Dr, John C Fox is a clinical psychologist. Dr John C. Fox **BSc (Hons.), D.Clin.Psy., PhD, AFsBPS, C.Psychol, FHEA. HCPC registered Clinical Psychologist** Director of Fox Psychological Services, advocates for the importance of healthy boundaries and individual autonomy, enmeshment, mental health and emotional well-bein.

Heidi Keller- Institute of Psychology, Osnabruck University,49069 Osnabruck, Germany (relatedness)

Reference to Emotional Boundaries.

[Remi Pearson, Founder of the Coaching Institute,- Meta Dynamics – Critical Alignment Model]

Speaker Bio

Bethsaida Hingston (born Bethsaida Flores Cabrera in 1971, Mexico) was raised by her parents, Filemón Flores Velasco and Lourdes Cabrera de Flores, whose wisdom and unwavering support instilled in her the values of resilience, kindness, and freedom. After marrying an Australian man, she became Bethsaida Hingston and continued to build her life around the principles her family taught her.

The loss of her father during the COVID-19 pandemic brought profound challenges, but the teachings of both her parents became her guiding light, helping her find freedom and inner strength.

Bethsaida has embraced vulnerability as a source of strength and found her purpose in helping others. She is a Life Coach, Founder of Betsy's Special Needs Services, and the author of *The Way to Freedom*. Her life's work honours her parents' legacy, turning challenges into opportunities for growth and inspiring others to discover their own paths to emotional freedom and resilience.

Notes

The Way to Freedom

Notes

The Way to Freedom

Notes

The Way to Freedom

Notes

www.ingramcontent.com/pod-product-compliance
Lightning Source LLC
Chambersburg PA
CBHW020414080526
44584CB00014B/1329